£3.90

QMW LIBRARY

D1492579

WITHDRAWN
FROM STOCK
QMUL LIBRARY

PUBLICATIONS OF THE DEPARTMENT OF
ROMANCE LANGUAGES
UNIVERSITY OF NORTH CAROLINA

General Editor: ALDO SCAGLIONE

Editorial Board: JUAN BAUTISTA AVALLE-ARCE, PABLO GIL CASADO, FRED
M. CLARK, GEORGE BERNARD DANIEL, JANET W. DÍAZ, ALVA V. EBERSOLE,
AUGUSTIN MAISSEN, EDWARD D. MONTGOMERY, FREDERICK W. VOGLER

NORTH CAROLINA STUDIES IN THE
ROMANCE LANGUAGES AND LITERATURES

ESSAYS; TEXTS, TEXTUAL STUDIES AND TRANSLATIONS; SYMPOSIA

Founder: URBAN TIGNER HOLMES

Editor: JUAN BAUTISTA AVALLE-ARCE
Associate Editor: FREDERICK W. VOGLER

Other publications of the Department: *Estudios de Hispanófila, Hispanófila,
Romance Notes, Studia Raeto-Romanica*

Distributed by:

INTERNATIONAL SCHOLARLY BOOK SERVICE, INC.
P. O. BOX 4347
Portland, Oregon   97208
U. S. A.

NORTH CAROLINA STUDIES IN THE
ROMANCE LANGUAGES AND LITERATURES
Number 141

THE VIBRANT SILENCE IN JORGE GUILLÉN'S
AIRE NUESTRO

131170
25/4/79

THE VIBRANT SILENCE IN JORGE GUILLÉN'S *AIRE NUESTRO*

BY

FLORENCE L. YUDIN

CHAPEL HILL

NORTH CAROLINA STUDIES IN THE ROMANCE
LANGUAGES AND LITERATURES
U.N.C. DEPARTMENT OF ROMANCE LANGUAGES

1974

WESTFIELD
UNIV.
LONDON
COLLEGE

Library of Congress Cataloging in Publication Data

Yudin, Florence L

The Vibrant Silence in Jorge Guillén's *Aire nuestro.*
(North Carolina Studies in the Romance Languages and Literatures,
no. 141) Includes bibliographical references.

1. Guillén, Jorge, 1893-   . Aire nuestro.
I. Title. II. Series.

PQ6613.U5A738   861'.6'2   74-16025
ISBN 0-88438-941-3

I.S.B.N. 0-88438-941-3

IMPRESO EN ESPAÑA
PRINTED IN SPAIN

DEPÓSITO LEGAL: V. 3.729 - 1974

ARTES GRÁFICAS SOLER, S. A. - JÁVEA, 28 - VALENCIA (8) - 1974

To the memory of my Father

This book speaks with several voices other than my own. I wish to thank especially Professors Frances W. Weber and James O. Crosby for their recreation of *Aire nuestro* and for the happy inventions of their thinking and sensitivity.

The publication of this book was made possible by a grant from the Florida International University Foundation, Miami, Florida.

CONTENTS

INTRODUCTION

Aire nuestro is Guillén's metaphor for the totality of human existence. We encounter our most real humanity through our own vibrant impulse of affirmation in the struggle to make and share a livable world. For those who would secure this alliance between self and reality, the overriding task is to increase awareness, to promote genuine relationship with the environment and society. *Aire nuestro* expresses in terms of intelligence and sensitivity the sustained dialogue which is consciousness and experience. It is, however, a poetry of correlations and contrasts, and thus it also explores the negation of life: the forces of violence, repression, and alienation reverberate in its counterpoint. Inertia and passivity oppose the creative impulse and must be resisted as inimical to awareness. The three component parts of *Aire nuestro*, entitled *Cántico, Clamor,* and *Homenaje,* record with differing perspectives the dialectics of human values.

Among the conditions which Guillén appreciates as indispensable to conscious existence, the qualities of silence have a comprehensive importance. They are as essential in *Aire nuestro* as companionship, dreams, or the attempt to find unity in diversity. Where life thrives, silence tinctures heightened awareness; conversely, in a de-humanized context, silence becomes cancerous. In one sense, Guillén's poetization of silence reiterates Max Picard's objections to abusive technology: "Silence has been banished from the world today... Silence seems to survive only as a mere 'structural fault' in the everlasting flow of noise." [1] But on a more

---

[1] Max Picard, *The World of Silence*, trans. Stanley Godman (Chicago: Henry Regnery Co., 1952), p. 92.

comprehensive level, Guillén's negative silences represent the self-imposed dehumanization of unthinking or insensitive lives.

In addition to social and ecological benefits, Guillén attributes a great creative potentiality to the modes of silence. Silence resounds in the world as a generative source of action and reflection, discovery and response. Its vibrancy in the text of *Aire nuestro* may be heard as an invitation to the reader's own creativity. Sartre has described beautifully how the intuitive silence of author and reader combine to re-invent the act of reading as an experience in "directed creation". For Sartre, the literary object "is by nature a silence and an opponent of the word." It is a diffuse texture whose weave depends on the reader's creative labor: "Nothing is accomplished if the reader does not put himself from the very beginning and almost without a guide at the height of this silence; if, in short, he does not invent it and does not then place there, and hold on to, the words and sentences which he awakens." [2] In two ways, Guillén's treatment of silence exemplifies the esthetic and human implications in Sartre's thought. The metaphors and imagery involving silence represent the attempt to re-discover the world without exclusive recourse to verbal signs: the experience of silence hones the intellect and the senses to the full resonance of reality. Like Sartre's sensitivity to the liabilities of language, Guillén's fresh insights convey the joy and respect the limitations of human utterance.

The purpose of this book is to explicate the signs and overtones which Guillén has so richly created for the world of silence. No attempt has been made heretofore to define comprehensively the contexts of a single motif in the 1,700 pages of Guillén's poetry. Although such an approach has been strongly recommended, the choice of contextual analysis as a principal procedure should and can be questioned. [3] Whatever one's criteria for analysis, there must exist indentifiable characteristics in the work which correspond to the method applied. Does *Aire nuestro*

---

[2] Jean-Paul Sartre, *Literature and Existentialism*, trans. Bernard Frechtman, 5th ed. (New York: The Citadel Press, 1969), p. 44. Sartre develops this point from other angles on pp. 14, 24-25, 37, 45, 57.

[3] Concha Zardoya, "*Clamor I*: Stylistic Peculiarities," trans. Bernice G. Duncan, in *Luminous Reality*, ed. Ivar Ivask and Juan Marichal (Norman: The University of Oklahoma Press, 1969), p. 175.

reveal a poetic idiom which depends on motif patterns and their contexts? And secondly, is there a structural unity which gives esthetic coherence to the three separate books, *Cántico*, *Clamor*, and *Homenaje*? The first question involves a decision about the importance of theme and context; the second touches upon the larger problem of how to understand Guillén's compilation of *Aire nuestro*.

Nearly every serious study of Guillén's poetry has brought to light some aspect of formal correspondence among the separate compositions. [4] No one has convincingly demonstrated that each independently published book stands apart from its predecessor or successor in Guillén's style and thought. Unless he intended to limit his remarks to certain preferences in narrative content, R. J. Weber's opinion that Guillén 'abandoned' the tenets of *Cántico* after 1948 does not stand the test of close reading in each of the three works. [5] It hardly seems possible to say that the poetry of *Clamor* and *Homenaje* resonates in a different modality from the original sounds of *Cántico*. Therefore, the question concerning the proposed analysis of a single motif and the creative integrity of the object to be examined comes to terms with the fundamental structure of *Aire nuestro*.

A significant area of this inter-relationship depends upon context. Guillén himself has selected this feature of his poetry as one of its most pervasive constants: "Everything depends upon context. The one thing that matters is the placing of each component within the whole, and this functional value is the one

---

[4] The question of unity with respect to *Cántico* and *Clamor* has been intelligently summarized by Andrew P. Debicki, "El *Cántico* de Jorge Guillén," in *Estudios sobre poesía española contemporánea* (Madrid: Gredos, 1968), pp. 112-114. Cf. Biruté Ciplijauskaité, "*Clamor* a la altura de las circunstancias," *RHM*, XXIX (julio, 1963), 290-297. The organic relationship of *Homenaje* with *Clamor* and *Cántico* has been discussed by the following: Andrew P. Debicki, "El tema de la poesía en *Homenaje*, de Jorge Guillén," *Insula*, XXIII (septiembre, 1968), 1; Ricardo Gullón, "*Homenaje* con variaciones," *Insula*, XXIII (septiembre, 1968), 1.

[5] Robert J. Weber, "De *Cántico* a *Clamor*," *RHM*, XXIX (abril, 1963), 109-119; cf. Jorge Guillén, "Introduction" to *Affirmation*: *A Bilingual Anthology*, 1919-1966, trans. Julian Palley (Norman: University of Oklahoma Press, 1968), pp. 18-24. Manuel Durán had previously set forth the basic assumption of Weber's argument, "Después de *Cántico*: armonías y estridencias de Jorge Guillén en *Maremágnum*," *RHM*, XXV (1959), 227-228.

that is decisive." [6] In support of this critical approach, the most attentive readers of *Aire nuestro* have identified the expressive range of the book's language through the analysis of thematic cores. [7] The internal order of Guillén's collected poetry depends upon multiple nuclei, or perspectivism, and this complexity shows thematic variation to be one of the most pivotal constants. To put it differently, the detection and interpretation of a single key theme in *Aire nuestro* will reveal a number of contextual components which unify the esthetic vision.

I have gathered all of the data on the contexts of silence in *Aire nuestro* with no pre-conceived notion of a system of classification. [8] Once such data had been isolated, however, I was able to see that silence, because it is a key theme in a large corpus of poetry, naturally had grown out of a specific conceptual core. This cluster has five main contexts: the association of silence with an ideal order or harmony; silence as a mediator in creative and intellectual activity; the qualities of silence in love and communication; negative silences; and silence as a metaphysical phenomenon. Finally, the analysis of each of the five contexts of silence must not be allowed to destroy the poet's own meticulous order of publication: *Cántico*, *Clamor*, and *Homenaje* will be treated as three formal divisions of *Aire nuestro*.

---

[6] "The Language of the Poem: One Generation," in *Language and Poetry* (Cambridge: Harvard University Press, 1961), p. 214.

[7] For useful commentary on the organic unity of Guillén's poetry, I am indebted to the following: Amado Alonso, "Jorge Guillén, poeta esencial," in *Materia y forma en poesía* (Madrid: Gredos, 1955), pp. 370-373; Dámaso Alonso, "Los impulsos elementales en la poesía de Jorge Guillén," in *Poetas españoles contemporáneos* (Madrid: Gredos, 1965), pp. 203-227; Joaquín Casalduero, *Jorge Guillén: "Cántico"* (Santiago: Cruz del Sur, 1946), pp. 55-69, et passim; Andrew P. Debicki, *Estudios*, pp. 113-134; Jaime Gil de Biedma, *"Cántico": El mundo y la poesía de Jorge Guillén* (Barcelona: Seix Barral, 1960), pp. 28-37, 128-137; Joaquín González Muela, *La realidad y Jorge Guillén* (Madrid: Insula, 1962), pp. 15-29, 201-223; Concha Zardoya, "Jorge Guillén: siete poemas en azar de perfección," in *Poesía española contemporánea* (Madrid: Guadarrama, 1961), pp. 286-334.

[8] There are over two hundred poems which contain references to silence: 76 in *Cántico*; 50 in *Clamor*; 78 in *Homenaje*. All quotations from Guillén's poetry refer to *Aire nuestro* (Milan: All'Insegna del Pesce D'Oro, 1968). Although my study will be limited to the contents of *Aire nuestro*, it is interesting to note additional contexts of silence in Guillén's most recent poetry: *Guirnalda civil* (Cambridge: Ferguson Press, 1970), pp. 27, 33; and "Nocturnos," Nos. 2, 4, in *Insula*, XXV (julio, 1970), 9.

I

HARMONIOUS SILENCE

For Guillén, the conditions of harmonious existence are to be found in the diverse phenomena of daily reality. Being in harmony involves the discovery of these conditions and the freedom to invent their modes. Harmony, then, is both a responsible choice and an act of creation. In *Aire nuestro* it is a matter of responsibility if one's actions are to support rather than to undermine the resources; it is creative in the sense that man locates his reality by responding to and becoming part of a potential accord. What is fundamental in this alliance, however, is man's perception of himself as both subject and object. Clearly, there can be no vital human experience unless he is aware of himself as an integral part of symbiosis. In this way the individual binds himself to the outside world and affirms his own identity. His individuality is neither absorbed nor egotistically isolated when he has perceived the inter-relatedness of all existence. Consequently, there is no problem of identity: 'I am out there, and with myself.'

In *Aire nuestro* harmony means self-realization. Silence accompanies this experience and sharpens its sensorial lines. Increased consciousness depends upon awareness of what is going on before, during, and after the experience of ourselves in the world. In these moments, silence radiates cues for the processes of change, growth, and inter-action. Guillén dramatizes the effects of silence on heightened awareness through a concerted stylistic effort. The synesthetic richness with which he endows its contexts enables the reader to hear, see, feel, and live silence as harmony. Light, contours, texture, and sound all contain or project silent charges.

Each experience of attentive participation, whether conceptual, intuitive, or abstract, results in an expanded awareness of man's cohesion with reality.

A. *Cántico*

In keeping with the dominant tone of *Cántico*, the highest concentration of referents for silence denotes affirmation. At the center of this cluster of meanings is the idea of coordination between man and the external world: "*Cántico* is formed of contemplation and action. Both are directed toward a single end: to intensify the consciousness, the wholeness of our being in the world." [9] To perceive and appreciate this alliance is to know the full joy of existence:

> Del silencio se levantan
> Murmullos: silencio... mío.
> Entre nieblas, entre sábanas
> Permanece elemental
> Una convicción. Se entraña
> Mi ser en mi ser. Yo soy...
> Follajes hay que resguardan
> Por entre el ruido y el fárrago
> Silenciosas enramadas.
> Todavía en el silencio
> Perduran nuestras palabras
> De mayor fe. ¿Las adviertes
> Bajo el ímpetu del ansia
> Por amar, cantar, saltar?... [10]

Silence is watched and listened to; it is perceived in its movement and stasis. Like the silently linked branches, insulated against background noise, the lovers in this poem individually share a silence which affirms their identity as a couple. The serene observer lives his co-substantiality with nature and his beloved. Confident that relationship thrives on change and renewal, the plenitude of self echoes in the ordered flux of the natural world.

----

[9] Jorge Guillén, "Introduction," *Affirmation*, p. 21.

[10] "Mundo en claro," 456:9, 461:17. For the reader's convenience, verse numbers will be supplied whenever the length of the poem cited exceeds twenty-five lines.

A parallel experience of uncomplicated well-being contains an image of silence in which the boundaries between 'now-ness' and 'us-ness' harmonize: "¡Oh continua, profunda suavidad de silencio! / La sangre corre. / ¡Pleno vivir henchido de presente aceptado! / Todo es ahora." ("Más esplendor," p. 413.) As awareness becomes more acute, the interrelationship of self and the surroundings also gathers intensity: "Asciende mi ladera / Sin alterar su acopio de silencio." (p. 175.) The multiple use of possessive pronouns underscores this accord, while the alliterations seem to echo the closeness. With a shift in perspective, the idea of harmonious awareness re-occurs in the poem, "El concierto" (p. 189). Guillén interprets the unfolding of a musical design as an archetypal experience: "El tiempo se divide resonando. / ¡Ah! Se levanta un mundo / Que vale, se me impone, me subyuga / Con su necesidad. / Es así. Justamente, / Según esta delicia de rigor, / Ha de ser en el aire: / Un mundo / Donde yo llego a respirar con todos / Mis silencios acordes." When the ego focuses outward there is no struggle to adjust to the on-going reality: clear perception recreates the musical pattern in terms of human harmony. With equal satisfaction, the close experience of 'soundless' order reinforces acceptance of the world as it is: "Y la vida, sin cesar / Humildemente valiendo, / Callada va por el aire, / Es aire, simple portento. / ...A una creación continua / —Soy del aire— me someto." ("El aire," pp. 520:5, 523:21.) The congruence of "aire" and "vida" in Guillén's poetic language is a metaphor for fusion. The two terms share the qualities of creative affirmation and simplicity; together, "aire" and "vida" represent perfect synchronism and dynamic continuity. Thus, silence designates the imminence of sufficiency; it is the pre-condition and an attendant circumstance of harmony. [11]

En multitud las estrellas,
Bellísimas aunque insomnes,

---

[11] Several critics have discussed the similarity between Guillén's concept of harmony and the Horatian ideal of unity: Casalduero, *Jorge Guillén*, pp. 33-41, et passim; Ricardo Gullón, "La poesía de Jorge Guillén," in *La poesía de Jorge Guillén* (Zaragoza: Heraldo de Aragón, 1949), pp. 62-74; Alfredo Lefebvre, *Poesía española y chilena* (Santiago, 1958), pp. 89-98; Luis Lorenzo-Rivero, "Afinidades poéticas de Jorge Guillén con Fray Luis de León," *CHA*, 230 (febrero, 1969), 421-436.

Allá lejos se abandonan
A su perfección: son orbes.
Hacia un silencio común
Gravitan. Nada responde,
Pero todo está. Conviven
Los astros con los alcores...

("Caminante de puerto, noche sin luna," p. 466:11)

The speaker in this poem shares the experience of harmony which music or well-being may mirror: equilibrium has lucid calm, tensioned peace, and the universe projects the same "delicia de rigor" described as esthetic pleasure in "El concierto." Guillén establishes this parallel in the proximity of the terms "orbes" and "perfección," while the verbal structure, "se abandonan," "gravitan," "está," and "conviven" assigns connotations of direction and order to the observed spectacle. Outer space is also animated: the void is filled with vibrant silence. The expressive overtones of silence in "El concierto," "El aire" and "Caminante de puerto, noche sin luna," derive from the single fact of unimpeded consciousness in rapport with the world around it. [12]

In many of the preceding texts silence functions as an indispensable element of harmony because the whole design of the poem concerns the experiences of a confident being. Because *Aire nuestro* is a poetry of contrasts and correlations, it is important to observe what happens to the role of silence in situations which are inherently more ambiguous or conflictive. The last poem in *Cántico*, "Cara a cara" (pp. 524-530), combines the motif of harmonious silence with the ever-present threats of destruction:

El agresor general
Va rodeándolo todo.
—Pues... aquí estoy. Yo no cedo.

(525:22)

¿Perdura el desabarajuste?
Algo se calla más hondo.
¿Siempre chirría la Historia?
De los silencios dispongo.

(530:21)

---

[12] Related examples of this context of silence in *Cántico* include the following: pp. 177:14, 246, 273, 366, 430:2, 434:2, 447, 495:7.

History teaches that there is an overlap between natural order and invented disorder. How does one accept this contradiction and strive for a paradoxical peace? The solution which Guillén proposes, and the point of view in the entire development of *Clamor*, excludes capitulation to the forces of negativity. Whatever contingencies splinter the wholeness of the self and the world upon which it depends must be confronted or undermined in acts of defiance. In this context, man is not defined by history or circumstance; rather, the human condition thrives and struggles to re-shape itself outside the net of inhuman events.

Besides the meanings of silence as a perennial source of harmony, there is an additional component which outlines Guillén's poetization. The qualities of silence have dynamic and concrete projection: by endowing silence with physical properties, it may inter-act with the surrounding objects, thus enhancing and activating the poem's texture. Through a process of fusion and objectification, silence is represented as a creative agent in the natural world. The way silence is perceived and translated by the spectator illustrates a pervasive sensorial focus in Guillén's vision. [13] In terms of thematic variation on silence, this fusion assumes, as does a metaphor, a double role. The properties of silence unify external phenomena and give cohesiveness to otherwise isolated data. Consequently, many synesthetic images of silence project harmony in the making.

In *Cántico*, the most characteristic fusion of silence involves the action of light. [14] This association offers a wide range of striking condensations. Silence may blend with other qualities,

---

[13] Gil de Biedma provides an excellent analysis of Guillen's perceptual techniques, "*Cántico,*" pp. 28-31. Cf. González Muela, *La realidad,* pp. 50-123. There is some disagreement among critics as to which of the senses dominates in Guillén's poetry: Casalduero, *Jorge Guillén,* pp. 96-97; González Muela, pp. 146-147; but the interplay of all sensory data is emphasized by the following: Dámaso Alonso, "Los impulsos elementales," pp. 220-234; Debicki, *Estudios,* pp. 30-33; C. B. Morris, "In Praise of Creation," in *A Generation of Spanish Poets, 1920-1936* (Cambridge: Cambridge University Press, 1969), pp. 119-142, et passim.

[14] See Amado Alonso's perceptive analysis of the contexts of silence and light in Neruda's *Residencia,* in *Poesía y estilo de Pablo Neruda* (Buenos Aires: Losada, 1940), pp. 223-224, 253-254. Héctor Giovannoni has studied carefully the radiation of this motif in "El silencio y la palabra en Leopoldo Panero," *CHA,* 231 (marzo, 1969), 681-694.

or cause its own immediate sphere of activity to become filled
with a new element: "¡Qué desgarrón de claridad / En el
silencio...!" (396:3); "Y en el silencio se cierne / La unanimidad
del día, / Que ante el toro estupefacto / Se reconcentra amarilla."
(489:7.) The melding of different luminosities produces a 'thick'
clarity: "Es una maravilla respirar lo más claro. / ... / Hasta el
silencio impone su limpidez concreta" ("Equilibrio", 318:1,9).
Perhaps the most dramatic fusion of silence and light occurs in
the sonnet, "La noche de más luna," (p. 292):

> ¡Oh noche inmóvil ante la mirada:
> Tanto silencio convertido en pura
> Materia, ya infundida a esta blancura
> Que es una luz aun más que una nevada!

The tight relationship among the nouns in this quatrain creates
a metaphoric chain reaction: qualities and forms meld in a single
projection of layered luminosity.

Complementing the images based on a fusion of silence and
light, other contexts add a spatial or tactile dimension. Silence is
conceived as a kind of 'chemical caress' which elicits equally
gentle responses from the matter it touches. In "Arena" (p. 492),
the beach is "suave de silencio" like the texture of a beautiful
evening. In another poem, "¿Ocaso?" (p. 328), night gathers this
silence into its folds: "...El silencio recibe en su alfombra / Los
sones menguantes del mundo." Silence interacts with the movement of water, and it creates a "quietud en tensión" ("Amplitud,"
p. 322). As a binding element, water marks its course silently:
"¡Qué serena va el agua! / Silencios unifica." ("Río," p. 506.)
Silence grows with the surrounding world and changes under
the influence of intense heat: "Un sol sin aleros, / Masa de la
tarde, / Convierte en silencio / De un furor el aire" ("El sedien-
to," p. 84).

The experience of silence, in any of its sense-awakening contexts, hones the percipient for responsiveness. As González Muela
notes, immersion in silence stimulates forgotten sensations: "Dos
minutos del silencio [la ocasión de la muerte del rey Jorge VI]...
Se empezaron a oler olores en los que uno no reparaba cuando
la ciudad estaba viva: olía a primavera presentida; y que se
oyeron ruidos como los que se oyen en la paz del campo..."

(*La realidad y Jorge Guillén*, p. 180). This recollection suggests the richness and drama which Guillén's conversions of silence produce in *Cántico*.[15] Silence spans full consciousness, and in *Aire nuestro* its metaphoric stretch nurtures enlightenment and plenitude.

B. *Clamor*

Cántico may be considered the most affirmative part of *Aire nuestro*, and *Clamor*, the most skeptical. In many ways, *Clamor* is the critical companion to the human and esthetic roots which it shares with its predecessor and its successor. The text of Guillén's second book derives its intensity from a sustained dialectical focus: ambivalence, violent change, and insecurity are pitted against their opposites, and the refractions of harmony filter through mock-dramatic scenarios or ironic discourse. Political sham and honest commitment are sometimes indistinguishable in the distortions of civil strife. But the poetry of *Clamor* faces with courage the real contradictions of life, and is poignantly wedded to re-humanization. Over and above the din of conflict, the word of greatest vigor also expresses the deepest silence. From the stridencies and truths of this poetry, a new synthesis emerges: chaos and order, harmony and dissonance ultimately lock together. In terms of the perspectivism of *Clamor*, neither order nor harmony has a fixed unidimensionality. Opposites may be no more than dislodged halves when viewed in the light of freedom and diversity.

In *Clamor*, the association between silence and equilibrium is thus very tenuous and more painfully attained than it was in the contexts of *Cántico*. A complementary variation appears in the distinct language and expressive modes which Guillén adopts for a silence whose very reality seems to be negated in the book's dominant tone. Whatever the situation which generates the dialectics of *Clamor*, responsibility and lucid enthusiasm for life defend *Aire nuestro* against self-destruction. The dramas of silence in *Clamor* suggest the horror but affirm the beauty of an all-too-human planet.

---

[15] Related examples of this context of silence in *Cántico*: pp. 62, 70, 179, 200:9, 221, 309, 321, 413, 424, 475.

24 THE VIBRANT SILENCE

As in *Cántico*, the organic relationship of man and the universe conditions the atmosphere of *Clamor*. Integrity and dependence are confirmed in the attentive experience of silence. The ability to project and absorb is a bridge to basic understanding: "—A mí me conmueve hasta el asordado, vago, / casi incorpóreo zumbido de un silencio en que, / sin confundirse ni fundirse, ahora mismo se / traban infinitas radiaciones conjuntas. Y todo / está con todo, alrededor de este hombre erguido / sobre la peña..." ("Atención a la vida," 933:6.) In order to express this fulfillment, it is unnecessary to reconcile opposites. Guillén's use of contradictory qualifiers, while suggesting simultaneity and differentiation, ironically conveys the sense of tensioned wholeness. The willingness to listen to the sounds of silence, to allow natural phenomena to make their sensorial imprint, is also the subject of "Una iluminación" (pp. 810-813):

> Desde el silencio o tras los apogeos
> De música,...
> La realidad manaba realidad,
> Y en torno ya asentándose
> Me declaraba centro verdadero
> De un orbe
> Para siempre salvado.
>
> (811:2, 812:4)

Silence is also represented as a basic knowledge which overlaps self-affirmation. The outward-looking ego discovers its balance by evenly distributing its focus. Often, this realization is followed by a concomitant understanding of change and pattern:

> La oscuridad y el silencio son una masa negativa que, sin embargo, cubre, pesa y me protege a mí,...
> El silencio va convirtiéndose en zumbido difuso como energía del negror donde sigo, entre hilachas de imágenes que tal vez esté soñando: blanda conciencia del aún molusco y ya persona.
>
> ("Vida concreta," p. 1040)

In the penumbra, opposites sketch their meeting point, and fragments are gathered into the incipient texture of a new day. The perception of this subtle fusing, as well as the acceptance of tension, announces emergence to full consciousness.

A related development of the inter-play between silence and self-affirmation shapes the dramatic climax in the poem, "Dimisión de Sancho," pp. 967-977:

> Amanece en silencio.
> El hombre
> Se descubre a sí mismo
> Despacio
> Mientras, una vez más,
> El sol consigue mundo.
> Y Sancho se levanta y calla, calla.
>
> (971:10)

The economy of language and the emphasis on transition reinforce the human predicament. Sancho emerges renewed from his crisis; instead of the trauma of dissociation, he is at last at one with his image. Like the sun's re-birth from the gestation of night ("El sol consigue mundo"), the original Sancho Panza grows out of the silent realization of his character:

> Tal porte silencioso
> Mueve a respeto, límites dibuja.
> Expectación. Los burladores, mudos,
> Dejan obrar a quien se impone, lento,
> Solo, desde su espíritu.
>
> (971:17)

What the previous night's silence has taught him, Sancho internalizes. The one who was toyed with now controls the moves; his opponents desist. Both the placement and the meaning of "expectación" function to set off the separate, reversed roles of the participants. "Expectación" is the brake on action, rather than a stimulus (see note 22). The distance between Sancho and the others is now frozen. The mockers have lost their victim, and stand awed before Sancho's self-mastery. With full dignity to Sancho, Cervantine irony is fixed in the closing noun, "espíritu."

In a lighter vein than "Dimisión de Sancho", the erotic fantasy, "El encanto de las sirenas" (pp. 595-599) repeats the action of silence on psychic re-adjustment. After the dreamer has indulged his need for excitement, he realizes the danger of too much fantasy: "Vanidades, callad. / Atroces las sirenas frente a frente.

Lo clamaba mi espanto. / ¡Silencio! Silencio mío a solas y cle-
mente" (599:1). Wild self-indulgence ("Vanidades") is more of
a threat than a satisfaction. When he regains his ordinary balance
("Silencio mío"), the protagonist understands that the exercise of
imagination does not require self-abuse. In the daylight of this
realization, he welcomes the "dama evidente" who unexpectedly
enters his cabin: "¡Plenitud de hermosura en desnudez! Ved sin
venda / La realidad en toda su leyenda." (599:27.)

It is one of the distinctive features of Guillén's poetry that
no mood or need of real people is considered outside his interest.
Humor, play, dreams, and loving accompany the need to understand the world, to find meaning in life, and to accept the limits
of humanity. "Silenciosamente," Guillén's most intense poem on
silence and identity, brings together some of man's deepest and
simplest thoughts:

> La tarde se contempla desde el monte
> Fijada con aplomo en el silencio.
> Silencio tan continuo da al espacio
> Tersura de materia, calma limpia,
> Profundidad de cauce donde fluye,
> Visible río largo, la corriente
> Del tiempo, de mi tiempo, de esta vida...
> Y se nos trasparenta ya un vacío,
> El último vacío en el silencio
> Claro, muy claro y simple donde corre,
> Se pierde, se nos pierde a nuestra vista
> —Aunque se salve y dure esta amplitud
> A través del silencio poseído
> Por alguien—nuestro curso condenado.
>
> (1056:1,18)

As silence joins the spatial and visual surroundings, as it is experienced in its poignant simplicity, it acts like a lens on the
landscape of life: reality, too, is of a piece. The contradictions
of life and death resolve themselves in the charted timelessness of
our being. Silence teaches a lesson in existentialism: the ineluc-
tible course of our lives toward nothingness is made up of a
seamless web, for nothing is lost, and no one excluded. Just as
the final silence is implied in the tangible experience of everyday,
so, too, death is knitted into the moments of optimum awareness.

With this balanced understanding, "Silenciosamente" carries both an acceptance of the idea of death and a rejection of absurdity.

In the contexts of silence and synesthetic imagery, *Clamor* like *Cántico* develops the theme in its harmonious and dynamic functions. One important difference to be noted is that the idea of formal perfection is viewed more as a problematic assumption than as a self-evident fact. In *Clamor*, poems such as "El acorde" (p. 551) and "Tréboles" (p. 984) still presuppose creative order: "Hacia el silencio del astral concierto / El músico dirige la concreta / Plenitud del acorde, nunca muerto"; "Noche perfecta sin un ruido / Que raye el perfecto silencio. / En Creación estoy sumido." While these two poems depict the cosmos in terms of beauty and order, other key contexts reflect uncertainty and contradiction. "Clamor estrellado" (p. 1079), the final poem in Guillén's second book, illustrates this shift in tone and focus:

> Creación que mal afronta la mente, inmensidad
> de astros y siglos nada vertiginosos para ese
> mar nocturno que surcan — como este planeta,
> entre constelaciones sumido en el silencio.

What has altered the idea of harmony is not the narrator's point of view but the disruptive intervention of "las explosiones y los disparos y / los murmullos" whose tumult means human suffering: "se funden a quejidos, gritos, / alaridos" (p. 1079:2). Yet despite the chaotic reality, the universe continues to recreate its inviolate order: "Algo se calla más hondo." As in "Cara a cara," the closing selection in *Clamor* affirms a reality beyond the reach of historical conflict. [16]

As the realization of harmony becomes more problematic, spatial and sensorial phenomena also shift out of focus. One such change involves the size and comprehensibility of the universe: "Hay tal soledad de silencio / Que me sume en sus espesores. / … / Mientras me confío al reposo / De una inmensidad tan enorme / Que sólo el silencio a estas horas / La abarca y en sí la recoge." ("A las tres, a las cuatro," p. 664.) Two silences; one impersonal, the other comforting. It is precisely this tension which

---

[16] Other contexts in *Clamor*: pp. 768, 893, 930, 970:11, 1025:22, 1035:14, 1053, 1063.

adds new perspectives in the context of harmony. Both silences come together and provide a center of security ("me confío al reposo") with respect to the world.

A comparable taking-in of the surrounding space serves as the theatrical backdrop for the opening scenes of "Huerto de Melibea." To make room for love, the garden seems to pull in its contours, to reduce the elements of chance: "Las voces y el silencio de la Tierra / Van fundiéndose en vasto / Rumor de fondo oculto. / El ansia enamorada así no yerra / Su término." (p. 901:18.) A mini-world forms to protect the lovers temporarily: "El huerto no es ahora más que hierba / Muy suave / Que sólo del gran pulso recóndito bien sabe / Mientras las ramas indistintas, dando / Toda su profusión a la negrura, / Se funden sin figura / Para asociarse al bando / de la invisible tierra, pero humana." (p. 907:15.) The silent order of the world and the impulse of two people are momentarily congruent: "Presente / Como una eternidad que entre los dos madura." (p. 902:11.) What will rupture this perfect alliance is not the breakdown of cosmic harmony but the introduction of human error.

C. *Homenaje*

As the title suggests, *Homenaje* is a poetry of recognition. Its contents reveal many of the poet's literary and intellectual affinities. Guillén turns his attention to the living past, to the literary "Aire nuestro" and its enduring humanity. Within this recreative frame, the theme of silence develops an additional function: the power to stimulate memory and to re-constitute forgotten experience. In the shared silence of literary creation, new meanings appear on the surface of old lines. Professor Gullón has drawn attention to the importance of this technique in the composition of *Homenaje*: "Los poemas llevan nombres que son referencias al vivir para crear, para crearse, para reconocerse al reconocerlos, al darlos por presentes en donde se sabe que están: en el silencio de la intuición y como voces de ese silencio mismo." [17] In Guillén's recall, the past is brought to re-connect with the vibrant present, and rather than being an abstract enactment, the tribute to life and literature takes the form of a live

---

[17] Ricardo Gullón, "*Homenaje* con variaciones," 1.

scenario. Poetry, friends, minds, and sensibilities are placed in the vital conjunction of their truth and our time. It is as if Guillén's admiration endowed them with a second life: in these models his own creativity finds a wealth of experience unmarred by time or death.

By respecting the silence of poetic intuition, Guillén tunes his writing to the enduring qualities of others. There are lessons to be learned and meanings to be revived in the conscious re-play of literary achievements. In the section entitled "Al margen," pp. 1091-1205, for example, the poems combine close translation with new readings. Guillén takes the reader to the threshold of someone else's intuition and scans the interior with his own unique insight. The results of this creative reading open up many pages of untapped wisdom. *Homenaje* suggests that we cultivate and recover our intellectual wholeness by speaking directly with the literature of the past.

In its restorative capacity, the motif of silence picks up the vibrations of lost harmonies. The exclamation, "Silencio: te adoro" (p. 1097), conveys appreciation for the wordless transitions which strengthen one's bonds with the world. There is a striving in the third part of *Homenaje* to reach these oases of silence: "Pausa callada profundiza el alba, / Y el insomne bendice con Cervantes / Este silencio, sí, 'maravilloso'." ("Más alba," p. 1630.) Silence bridges psychic distance; it spans transitions from weariness to enthusiasm:

> Rehacer estos órganos de vida fatigosa,
> Volver a las raíces, a su vigor nutricio,
> Creer en el silencio de esa noche estrellada,
> Dormir dormir, dormir para resucitar.
>
> ("Confianza," p. 1627)

In Guillén's sensitive translation of Valéry's poem, "El cementerio marino" (pp. 1494-1500), this association of silence and re-birth is expressively rendered:

> Sí, mar, gran mar de delirios dotado,
> Piel de pantera y clámide calada
> Por tantos, tantos ídolos del sol,
> Ebria de carne azul, hidra absoluta,
> Que te muerdes la cola refulgente

En un tumulto análogo al silencio,
’   El viento vuelve, intentemos vivir.

(1499:19)

In the thunderous silence (the inaudible tumult), new life reaches
the shore: "¡A revivir en la onda corramos!" (1499:18.)

The fresh perceptions which emerge from Guillén's literary
recreations complement the synesthetic images in the poetry of
Clamor and *Cántico*. As a complement to discovery, the central
poetic figure radiates unexpected qualities on the surrounding
elements, and the fusions of silence and natural phenomena which
I have studied thus far become even more susceptible of dynamic
effects in *Homenaje*. Our keenest attention is called to observe
the fascinating action of flux, harmony, and metamorphosis. The
world is "...leve / de silencio" (p. 1253), adorned by natural
surprise: "Sorpresa al despertar. Silencio: nieve" (p. 1253). A
"profundísimo silencio de universo" suggests multiple fusions,
harmony in diversity. This osmosis of qualities serves as the
poetic nucleus in "Fusión de silencio y luz" (p. 1630):

> Este silencio, riguroso ahora
> Como una pausa inviolable, junta
> Su reserva y su espera en vilo a una alba
> De blancos grises que el azul invocan
> Desde este corredor en que se funden
> — Todos duermen — la luz y este silencio.

Silence undergoes a material and a chromatic transformation;
it fills the early dawn and gathers into its own texture the hues
and mass which touch it. But sometimes the appearance of contrast
impinges upon our ability to see the underlying harmony: "¿El
silencio produce su aparición sonora? / ¿Se identifican ser y
nada?" ("Silencio en el origen," p. 1253.) Tension brings together
the separate phases of change and stasis, and the contradictory
meanings of "silencio" and "aparición sonora" designate a new
reality: opposites mesh; plurality is. [18]

---

[18] Similar contexts in *Homenaje*: pp. 1213, 1222, 1237, 1249, 1277, 1374,
1463, 1499-1500, 1503, 1507, 1511, 1561, 1623, 1627.

II

CREATIVE SILENCE

In the poetry of Jorge Guillén, "La atención es un éxtasis" (p. 323) because we grasp and recreate the world in acts of lucid intensity. The achievement of heightened awareness follows conscious involvement and exploration. It is neither self-transcendence nor mindless immersion. Critics have observed the important role of attention in *Cántico*, but, while many poems in *Clamor* and *Homenaje* also describe this joy in perception, it has not been observed as a dominant theme and focus. [19] Often, these poems are themselves containers for the process and result of inspired awareness. Guillén directs his art to the specific kinds of telescoping which precede insight, understanding, and adequate expression.

Just as harmony develops through symbiosis, creative acts depend on fusion and correspondence. There are no isolated or unique projects for creative living. Writing, loving, thinking or doing occur in a single sphere of human engagement. Whether the object produced is an image or an act, the ability to maintain a vibrant level of consciousness makes possible the achievement. In *Aire nuestro,* because the potential to create depends only upon man's free alliance with concrete reality, there is virtually no limit to the creative acts to be enjoyed simply by recognizing their imminence in the world. And that recognition often has a silent reflector.

---

[19] Dámaso Alonso, "Los impulsos elementales," pp. 211-214; Gil de Biedma, pp. 37, 61, 122-135; González Muela, pp. 123-124, et passim. Guillén's remarks on the subject of awareness and attention are very pertinent, "Introduction," pp. 5-7.

The presence of silence is itself a blueprint for creative experience. By watching how silence activates the surrounding phenomena, the observer frees his creative impulse. He is, so to speak, inside and around the process which precedes understanding and enjoyment. To know how to look at the world, to let speech, silence, memory, or image delineate hidden and obvious signs, is to possess a permanent artistic medium for infinite creative acts.

A. Cántico

"A mind awakens in a context of harmony... When health and freedom are sufficient, man affirms himself by affirming Creation..." [20] Without these two conditions, there can be no perception or possession of the creative potential. In *Aire nuestro*, to be freely dependent upon reality is to belong to the process of creativity: "No soy nada sin ti, mundo. Te necesita / La cumbre de la cumbre en silencio: mi estupor." (p. 257.) The contexts of harmony reveal the wonder of the world as it is:

> ¡El aire! Vendaval o viento o brisa,
> Resonando o callando, siempre existe
> Su santa desnudez. ¿No la divisa
> Con los ojos de un dios hasta el más triste?
>
> ("Anillo," 183:17)

Daily observation and rapport make the discovery of the world always new. In this poem, as in the title and meaning of Guillén's collected poetry, "el aire" is a precious source of energy. In any of its degrees of presence ("vendaval," "viento," or "brisa"), and, because it is both movement and form, "el aire" is a metaphor for creative impulse. But it is man's unique ability to internalize this creative impetus ("los ojos de un dios"). Acute perception finds order and delight in its ordinary field of vision: "¡Con la esencia en silencio / Tanto se identifica!" ("Más allá," I, 27:23.) The conscious effort to enjoy the full span of sensory impressions inspires an observer with the beauty of his own creative attention: "¡Dulces silencios! A veces se habla / Solo en voz alta. / ... / ¡Mío es el mundo!" ("Interior," 216:7.) It

---

[20] Jorge Guillén, "Introduction," p. 4.

is in this joint action that Guillén's words, "man affirms himself by affirming Creation," resonate most brilliantly.

Silent ripeness for experiencing the world nurtures a basic confidence: "El verde al silencio adora. / ... / Respirar es entender, / ¡Cuánta evidencia en la atmósfera!" ("La isla," 495:10;17.) With another person, this trust deepens mutual awareness:

> Sin voces todavía,
> No deja de avanzar,
> De prosperar el diálogo
> Por la clara llanura
> Donde nuestros destinos
> Profundizan su propia libertad,
> A sus anchas en nuestro infatigable
> Convivir, trabajado
> Siempre por la atención.
>
> ("El diálogo," pp. 142-143)

The subtle progress of human relations sketches its creative impulse in silent interludes. Often, the absence of words is the most effective communication: "Hay lenguaje en la pausa / Que lo recoge silenciosamente, / A una intención denuncia / Su presentida sombra." ("El diálogo," 141:11.) In several of Guillén's love poems, silent prefaces and unspoken pauses are as concretely a part of sharing as the reticent words or acts of love. Time and continuity seem to meld in the vibrancy of conjunction: "Atención nada más de buen amigo. / Nació ya, nacerá. ¡Infiel, la gloria! / Mejor el buen silencio que consigo / Resguarda los minutos sin historia." ("Vida extrema," II, 403:21.) The rhythm of human closeness surpasses time.

The unspoken creativity of two people has a corresponding role in esthetic contexts. For the writer in *Aire nuestro*, timelessness silently announces the life of a poetic idea: "Mi secreto inhábil / Entre los relojes / Calla tan inmóvil / Que apenas si late." ("El prólogo," p. 41.) The action of silence on sensitivity opens new doors of insight. Following the reality of his interaction with the world, the poet can isolate creative sources:

> A solas mi silencio
> Se entiende con su valle.
> Sé de unas hermosuras
> Tan vivas, tan reales

Que sólo aquí me entregan
Su palabra, su clave.

("Tierra y tiempo," p. 478)

In the achievement of verbal art, silence is the opposite of non-language: it creates the before and after of poetic utterance. [21]

B. *Clamor*

In a contrastive statement on the underlying difference between *Cántico* and *Clamor*, Guillén has pointed out one of his centers of interest in *Aire nuestro*: the counterpoint in which tension and serenity vie for control: "deforming and destructive influences constitute the chorus of *Cántico*, a minor chorus of voices, secondary with respect to the singing voice. Near or remote, they remain in the background, quite capable of figuring as protagonists. Such they will be on other stages, and with such robust accents that they will form a 'clamor'." ("Introduction," p. 18.) As an atmospheric presence in the second book of *Aire nuestro*, static, dissonance, and acoustic discharge swell. Guillén often describes these "protagonists" as invaders; they block out the life of harmony and create a battle zone in the human consciousness. *Clamor* proposes a struggle against these deadening factors: whether the negative force be an ideology or a mechanized pollutant, the task is re-humanization. From this angle, Guillén's poetry makes clear how precious wholesome silence can be for the besieged world. In *Clamor*, vibrant silence is an island of awareness where the sensibilities can recover their creative potential.

While the space and sounds of *Clamor* designate a problematic vista, the willingness to experience the world with a free consciousness has an even greater urgency than *Cántico*. The more events and conflict encroach on the personal world, the greater the effort required to defend individual humanity. For Guillén, each new day provides the potential for self-realization:

---

[21] Related examples of this context in *Cántico*: pp. 142, 153, 154, 172, 292, 325, 514, 518-523.

Pálida luz por las rendijas.
Dulce expectación en silencio.
Sea, sol, lo que tú me elijas.

("Tréboles," 628:1)

From the lessons of his own renewals, the spectator at an aquarium
understands how all organisms share in re-birth: "Peces, peces...
A fuerza de silencio / Me dicen creación / En Creación ma-
yúscula,..." ("Una exposición," III, 772:1.) Mirroring in sharper
focus the invitation to be part of the plenitude at daybreak ("Único pájaro," *Cántico*, p. 257), the imagery of "Vida entera" (p. 690)
leads to a comparison of creative existence and daybreak:

Las aves enmudecen. Es más honda
Como una espera nuestra el alba muda
Bajo su libertad no decidida.
Tránsito corto. Va a sonar la onda
Que a las distancias en conjunto muda.
Pesará al sol de hoy la entera vida.

The burst of day —fusion of silence and sun— has a promise and
a finality: each dawn is unique, and the options opened are bound
by 'once-ness.' The possibility that one's hopes will be realized is
imminent in each new day ("Es más honda / Como una espera
nuestra el alba muda"), provided one seize the time (" 'Carpe
diem', así lo entiende Horacio —", 690:7). In the metaphor which
compresses expectation and silence, there is an implied optimism
despite the fragility of individual existence: for the speaker,
dawn's silence reverberates with creative anticipation; every dawn
is like a mini-life, and is more precious because unique. This is
the meaning conveyed in the last verse: 'Life in its entirety will
bear upon today's sun.' [22]

Close attention to what has already been created bears upon
the ability to recreate. In the resistance to hostile circumstances
there is an impulse to re-construct the inspirations which art has
preserved: "Silencio al fin. Escuchad / Como lo escuchó Cervantes." ("Tréboles," p. 1018.) From this respectful attentiveness

---

[22] I wish to thank Professor J. B. Avalle-Arce for suggesting that there
was a connection to be made in Guillén's use of "expectación" and silence
in "Dimisión de Sancho," "Vida entera," and "Huerto de Melibea." See
pp. 25, 47.

to past and present creative processes, new acts of insight may be generated. Among the poems whose re-discovery yields the deepest tonalities, Guillén singles out the *Coplas* of Manrique. The modern poet's understanding re-activates the human and literary values embedded in the poetic past:

> Se insinúa una música. La oigo
> Como un canto indistinto del silencio
> Mientras resurgen, tácitas, ingrávidas,
> Aquellas no ya vidas
> A la vez en su instante más vivaz
> —Yo también lo comparto—
> Y en un tiempo concluso,
> Que esta resurrección devuelve a un aire
> Traspasado de sol. El sol me alumbra
> Lo que vive no siendo en la frontera
> Más temporal, muy próxima a las lágrimas.
> Ahí
> Siento ahora inmortales
> A los que sé yacentes.
>
> ("Aquellas ropas chapadas," 761:15)

Esthetic and psychological time survive oblivion. The poem itself is the process whereby the past re-enters the zones of fresh appreciation. The tension between concrete and abstract reality, between historical time and contemplation, gives these verses the immediacy of live experience. Poetic art has the power to bring forth life in "recuerdos".

The poignancy of emotive projection in *Clamor* also converts private recollection into vital presences: "A veces te vivo en mí / Con tal embeleso aún / Que resucita el que fui." The poem is an act of love and the repository of its untapped energies. Just as "palabra," "clave" ("Tierra y tiempo," p. 478) emerge from silent gestation, the 'pastness' of love may be snapped by re-naming its essence: "Tú en el silencio de tu sombra. / Tendido sobre noche larga, / Yo en el silencio que te nombra." ("Tréboles," pp. 824-825.) In the poetry of *Clamor* this recaptured emotion alleviates the pain of loss and isolation; it opens up new possibilities for continual involvement:

> Amor, futuro sin ninguna linde,
> Coloquio en incesante crecimiento.
> Las palabras ya dichas no se pierden,

Y desde su pasado nos alumbran
Más espaciosas comunicaciones,
Entre medias palabras y clarísimos
Silencios.

("Tú más allá," 828:1)

The fact that such experiences overcome the contingencies of disorder and meaninglessness is at the core of Guillén's wisdom in *Clamor*. The creative impulse defies the forces of de-humanization: "Mientras el día repleto / De ruidos produce escoria, / Tú vives en el secreto / De la callada memoria." ("Culminación," p. 840:1.) One escapes the trap of events in order to become whole again. In this endeavor, as in the artist's task, silence offers the lucidity and calm for the creative preservation of life's most human moments.

C. *Homenaje*

Veneration for the written word and for the communication of what would be lost without the heritage of literature outline the conception of *Homenaje*. [23] The essence of what each poet has brought to expression — his imagination and creative impulse — becomes the new levels of reality on which later generations will build. Nothing is lost or poetically frozen in the inspired landscape. For Guillén, it is the leap we make to receive the poet's inspiration which gives impetus and truth to our own creativity. Several poems in *Homenaje* enact this participation in the living history of poetry; they are one writer's contribution to the joint efforts of an artistic community which in turn will generate new lines of communication and awareness.

Guillén's tribute to Azorín (pp. 1502-1505) traces the steps to realization of another's poetic world. It is an invitation to participate in the human adventure which a good writer has lived: "Del silencio — profundo silencio común — se elevan / las palabras." (1504:8.) At the height of this common silence, we can begin to perceive the poet's creative position. This is why shared recitation, as an alternative to private reading, has the advantage

---

[23] This theme has been thoughtfully examined by Andrew P. Debicki, "El tema de la poesía en *Homenaje*," and by Ricardo Gullón, "*Homenaje con variaciones*," 1, 6, 16.

of living context: with an interlocutor, one's discovery of a poet's original insight reaches out to connect with immediate response, and the silence of awakened sensibilities is twice as receptive: "Y más silencio prolonga, hondo, hen- / chido, el homenaje al poeta." (1505:20.) Silence is a bridge over which one vision enters another. Guillén sees the poet's task in terms of this sharing and its preservation of expressive value: "Los dos amigos callan. Recreándose en aquellas / imágenes de otra atmósfera..." (1504:1.)

To complement his appreciation of verbal art, Jorge Guillén respects the limits of language. His own silences and explicit emphasis on the intuitive links in writing are an integral part of his tribute to poetry. The poem, when left to its internal magic, reaches multiple layers of consciousness. With characteristic irony, Guillén describes the role of verbal un-reason in teasingly simplistic terms:

> El cacto medita y disiente.
> "Esto no está claro" me objeta
> Quizás el más noble lector.
> Bien puede ser. ¡Hay tal candor
> En el misterio del poeta!
> Algo ilumina la palabra.
> ¿Todo en silencio se oscurece?
> Si es preciso, di "abracadabra".
> Silencio: fondo torpe, trece.
>
> ("Sobre el silencio, la palabra," p. 1573)

Obviously, poetry will suffer from pseudo-explanation. What is needed is an open consciousness so that the reader can experience the freshness of poetic insight. The task for the writer is the same: to give expression to his creative impulse he must re-kindle the sensibility which preceded speech:

> Oscuridad, vacía falsamente.
> Inmerso todo en tácita sustancia,
> A la tiniebla invade· nuestra mente,
> Y el negror se reduce a resonancia
> De una memoria bajo luz sapiente.
>
> ("El mundo cabe en un recuerdo," p. 1628)

Guillén's dedication to the human meaning of poetry makes it clear why he would lament the silencing of poetic voices that sought to articulate new levels of awareness. To the poet whose artistic vision re-instated forgotten and unspoken realities, Guillén addresses his most impassioned tribute:

> Un murmullo cruzando va el silencio
> Con fluencia continua,...
> Que dice...
>   Dice: vida...
> Estalla claridad,
> Claridad que es humana
> Con su luz de conquista,
> Avance de una forma,
> De un gesto que es lenguaje,
> Triunfo de creador,...
>
> ("Federico García Lorca," p. 1289:1)

Lorca's commitment to the communication of human values fills the silence of his death, just as Pasternak's literary truth reverberates over the tundra of conformism: "Entre las nieves yace la solitaria brasa / Que no apagan las nieves, silencios sin ceniza. / ¿Callar es un martirio? Señas a solas mudas / En papel invisible no son gestos de loco. / La palabra se salva, sostiene vivo al hombre." ("Al margen de Pasternak," p. 1188.) Collaboration with these voices multiplies humanity's chances for creative survival. By experiencing another's heightened perceptions, each of us nourishes the potential for individual fulfillment:

> Sobre el silencio nocturno
> Se levantan, se suceden
> Frases. Las impulsa un ritmo:
> Claro desfile de versos
> Que sin romper el negror
> De la noche a mí me alumbran.
> Se funden cadencia y luz:
> Palabra hacia poesía,
> Que se cumple acaso en ti,
> En tu instante de poeta,
>   Mi lector.
>
> ("Tentativa de colaboración," p. 1595)

Silence, the wise mediator, disposes contingencies for dynamic lucidity: the human condition awakens to the pulse of a new rhapsode. [24] In the poetry of *Homenaje*, allied with Guillén's respect and admiration for the work of others, there is a trust in the nature of man. *Homenaje* praises all the human endeavors in which man's freedom becomes his creative source.

---

[24] This poem bears comparison with Guillén's delightful advice "Al amigo editor," p. 1557.

III

LOVE'S SILENCE

The experience of love occupies the center of Guillén's enlightened vision. Awareness, sensitivity, and understanding come to their most perfect fruition in love. [25] Love is neither a negation of the self nor a possession of the other: each partner most completely possesses his own reality in relationship with the other. Love thrives in conscious renewal and change; its tenuousness and its energy mesh like the words and acts of its expression. In his focus on love, Guillén avoids the extremes of reductionism and ideality: love does not define a simple physical union nor an all-inclusive rapport. When consciousness has been allowed to grow on many different and unequal levels, love creates a layered awareness in which mind and body are free to synchronize. The real limits of a shared life are respected, and the potential for growth and enthusiasm discovers its direction. The experience of love by an open sensibility is a concentration on the present: without sealing the past or refusing to structure the future, love finds its vibrant time in the now which is 'us-ness.' But the strength

---

[25] Gil de Biedma has written the most penetrating commentary on love in "*Cántico*," pp. 50-61. Cf. Dámaso Alonso, "Los impulsos elementales," pp. 210-225; González Muela, pp. 32-54, 146-171; Casalduero, pp. 147-150, 154-159. The contrast between Guillén's amorous poetry and the general tendency among his contemporaries can be best appreciated in C. B. Morris' valuable survey, pp. 61-69, 127-128, 163-170, et passim. Many contrastive features could also be drawn from Paul Ilie, *The Surrealist Mode in Spanish Literature* (Ann Arbor: University of Michigan Press, 1968), pp. 53-79, 121-130, 177-192, and Concha Zardoya, *Poesía española del 98 y del 27* (Madrid: Gredos, 1968).

of this immediacy implies a future because trust and responsibility protect the life that has been jointly created.

The confidence in human relations which is at the core of love in *Aire nuestro* derives from an understanding of the basic similarity of human nature, and it implies a willingness to affirm that likeness. Since love is the most compelling denial of difference, men and women can be equals in their truest moments. Thus Guillén rejects artificial male-female categories. There is no inherent conflict between the sexes; no intellectual blurring to mask the common desires and needs. Love relationships grow into and out of the space of *Aire nuestro,* so that times of withdrawal and insulation are just as natural as gregariousness and sharing in city life. The symmetry and openness which Guillén reserves for love make it a model for his entire conception of how man can promote his deepest alliance with the world.

I have found in the writings of Anaïs Nin striking parallels to this expression of love. [26] As a poetic novelist and a perceptive modern critic, Nin, like Guillén, concentrates on the creative potential of loving. Both writers telescope the moments of intensity which eliminate role-playing. They single out the contacts of interlocking sensibilities in a timeless harmony. The novelist's scenarios and the poet's images celebrate the moment when, as Nin put it, "we could create one another." (*The Novel of the Future,* p. 74.) For these two writers love is surcharged with beautiful silences. Shared silence rings with the surroundings and opens love's eyes to life-in-the-making. Above all, passionate silence generates the energy for two people to reach beyond separateness to integrity.

A. *Cántico*

Plenitude is 'us-ness': "¡Amor! Ni tú ni yo, / Nosotros, y por él / Todas las maravillas / En que el ser llega a ser." ("Salvación de la primavera," III, 105:5.) In this context of shared

---

[26] Anaïs Nin's ideas and analysis of love are most accessible in *The Diary of Anaïs Nin,* 3 vols., ed. Gunther Stuhlmann (The Swallow Press and Harcourt, Brace, and World, 1966-1969). See her excellent esthetic commentary in *The Novel of the Future* (Collier Books: Canada, 1970), pp. 44-56, 74-76, et passim.

otherness, silence outlines the lovers' closeness: "Henos aquí. Tan próximos, / ¡Qué oscura es nuestra voz! / La carne expresa más. / Somos nuestra expresión." (106:5.) Like the fusion of terms in a metaphor, the creation of a new 'voice' out of two separate idioms asserts its impulse through sensory association. The couple experiences the height of well-being, and consciousness expands to a sharper receptivity:

> Desde arriba, remotos,
> Invulnerables, juntos,
> A orillas de un silencio
> Que es abajo murmullos,
>
> Murmullos que en los fondos
> Quedan bajo distancias
> Unidas en acorde
> Sumo de panorama,
>
> Vemos cómo se funden
> Con el aire y se ciernen
> Y ahondan, confundidos,
> Lo eterno, lo presente.
>
> A oscuras, en reserva
> Por espesor y nudo,
> Todo está siendo cifra
> Posible, todo es justo.
>
> (VI, 110:5)

These verses might be taken as a synthesis of the love experience which crowns *Aire nuestro*. Wholeness of self and the other blends into the integrity of the world ("acorde sumo de panorama"). Acuteness of sensation ("remotos, invulnerables... a orillas de un silencio") suggests a consciousness ("lo eterno, lo presente") in which time releases its grip to the unifying force of love. Many of the human meanings which Guillén assigns to the term "aire" converge in the single image, "vemos cómo se funden con el aire." In this poem, the impulse which "aire" represents permeates and echoes human joy. On yet a different level, the impression of being one with the world is reinforced syntactically by the placement of "Todo" and "cifra" and in the proximity of ser-estar: "Todo está siendo cifra." The final verses of "Salvación de la primavera" convey Guillén's attitude to the centrality of awareness in everyday life: "Todo es justo" anywhere that thought and sensation create sufficiency for being alive.

The adequacy and normality of love are most fully developed as themes in "Sol en la boda" (pp. 158-165). While there is more irony and less lyric condensation in this poem, it is an outgrowth of the main ideas in "Salvación de la primavera." The psychological time of love ("los dos eternos siempre juveniles"), and the achievement of harmony through silent conviction are important markers in the poetic movement:

> Su plenitud consuman los compases
> En una sucesión nupcial que enlaza
> Los destinos de quienes, voz sin frases,
> Niegan el caos, vencen su amenaza.
>
> (II, 161:21)

The strength of their love can meet contradiction and chance. Similarly, the rejection of romantic illusions, and the delight in the adventure of normality protect and invigorate their future love:

> ¿Sumiso? No se engañan. Saben todo
> Lo muy terrestre que será su ruta,
> Rica de recta simple y de recodo
> Quizá a merced de una intemperie bruta.
>
> (163:9)

The idea that fulfillment is the daily task and not a result of wishful thinking, underlies their confidence:

> Instantes, horas, días en que el hombre
> Se embriaga de ser. ¡Ah, ser en pleno
> Con tal actualidad que el ser asombre!
> Lúcida embriaguez sin mal ni freno.
>
> (162:13)

To be 'high' on life, the couple must create a context for its expansion. Embedded in this core of heightened experience there is a silent understanding: the strength of love depends on clear signals exchanged by two people who authenticate their commitment:

> Jugadores, arriesgan: van gozosos.
> ¡Cuánto supuesto en su silencio denso!

¡Tan callados, tan cómplices, qué esposos!
Ceremonia. Posible hasta el incienso.
(164:13)

Love's silence is a deep complicity which resounds with the sum of joint acts. [27]

Although silence nurtures love relationships in *Cántico* and characterizes the dominant attitude in which the woman is remembered, Guillén does not transform this portrayal into an abstraction. It is the real presence of the beloved and the dialogue of unspoken affection which produce the vitality of love: "Sabes callar. Me sonríe, / Amor, desnuda tu boca." ("Invocación," p. 497.) Introspection becomes superfluous in the silence of being loved. Such sharing on a non-verbal level overlaps and softens the intervals of separation:

> Sólo tú,
> Siempre lejos
> En secreto,
> Calmas
> Lo azul demasiado azul.
> Gárrulas encrucijadas
> Del día: el sol
> En las bocas.
> Para tu amor hay noche: silencio a la redonda
> De tu voz.
> ("Siempre lejos," p. 303)

Silence mediates the transition from the sounds and intensity of daytime to the nocturnal alliance of tender tranquility.

B. *Clamor*

It is to be expected that as a protest against de-humanization and repression *Clamor* should introduce meanings of silence not found in the love poetry of *Cántico*. Equally consistent with the compilation of *Aire nuestro* is the development and expansion of

---

[27] Two similar instances of the insulating presence of silence in a love relationship occur in "Los amantes," p. 47 and "A pesar de todo," p. 326. See the conflicting opinions on the meaning of this silence proposed by Casalduero, pp. 141-156, 177-179, González Muela, pp. 147-156, Dámaso Alonso, p. 225, and Concha Zardoya, "Jorge Guillén: siete poemas," pp. 301-302.

context. Several of the longest and most intense poems in this
book reveal a tight correspondence with Guillén's first-published
work.

Refractions of love's sufficiency play on the surface of *Clamor*
like a motif from *Cántico* which is still structurally important.
The simplicity and self-realization which support the love relationship continue to occupy Guillén's creative attention: "...Hubo
algún jardín / Con viales de silencio. / Hubo la ciudad pequeña
/ Donde el presente es recuerdo. / ... / Las pasiones / De los
dos aparecieron / De pronto sumadas. Somos / La suma. Destino quiero." ("Conciencia de la suma," p. 1062:15.) Love's
impulse transforms the most ordinary rush-hour scene into a pedes-
trian's paradise. Its vital simplicity and human drama counteract
the city's anonymity. As in "Salvación de la primavera," the lover
moves out of a chaotic setting towards his most real adventure
with life:

> Le esperaban sus máximas verdades,
> Su gloria silenciosa:
> Amor
> Que, si no mueve el sol ni las estrellas,
> Blanco supremo da a la vida humana.
>
> ("Cita," V, 948:16)

The soft irony underscores the ordinariness and thrust of love's
impetus, while the words "verdades" and "gloria" shift the emphasis to the level of ideals. The din which explodes in this poem
as "Universal estruendo" and "superflua algarabía" (p. 945), dis-
solves in the human silence of the final verses. [28]

"Huerto de Melibea" (pp. 898-917) is perhaps the most lyrically
sustained love poem in *Aire nuestro*; it is also the most elaborate
dramatization of one of Guillén's strongest beliefs, the opposition
of life against death. Rojas' words, "Todo por vivir" are indeed
the best epigraph for Guillén's enactment of the play's climax. The
poem opens with a delicate lyric prologue in which the scene and
sense of Rojas' dramatic world are recreated: "Del instante en
silencio parten hacia lo oscuro / Las fuerzas que se acrecen de-
seando, / Formando su futuro: / El mando / Que habrá de

---

[28] Cf. Andrew P. Debicki, "Los detalles cotidianos en 'A la altura de las
circunstancias'," in *Estudios,* pp. 135-149.

presidir el mediodía." (898:1.) The action of silence imitates the indulgent touches of a gracious *tercera*, whose task it is to provide the best conditions for love: "Escucha. / No se oye nada. / Todo se vuelve desierto / Para proteger tu amor." (901:5.) "La noche" follows Lucrecia's observation with additional details on the progress of silent fusions which protect the lovers: "Las voces y el silencio de la Tierra / Van fundiéndose en vasto / Rumor de fondo oculto. / El ansia enamorada así no yerra / Su término." (901:18.) Later, the protagonists enjoy the vibrations of silence as if they were duplicates of their own desires:

C.   ¡Silencio!
M.   Escucha.
C.   Calla, calla.
M.   ¿Qué dices? No te oigo.
       Dímelo bien, más cerca del oído.
C.   Del oído.

(904:2)

A long transition follows their dialogue of love in which "La Noche", functioning as a prophetic voice, suggests the imminence of tragedy: "Amor, de amor capaz, / —Si no lo arrasa todo con el oculto filo / De pronto violento— / Extiende este sigilo / De paz." (908:11.) Up to this point, silence represents the participatory calm of the natural world: while harmony is sustained by the lovers' affirmative impulses, the universe seems to confirm and foster their union. But as soon as Calisto breaks the pattern of reasonableness, the stage is transformed from the garden of Eros to death's threshing floor:

No oigo bien el murmullo de esa fuente.
Corre tanto el destino
De algunos seres a su desenlace
Que en el silencio se precipita de repente
La expectación del mundo.

(913:15)

Calixto's precipitous action is a metaphor for a dashed future. The sparse verbs in these lines, "corre", "se precipita", mark off the substance of a key statement. While cosmic intervention is admitted ("el destino"), the other nouns in this assertion suggest human error: "seres," "desenlace," "expectación," and "mundo."

Unlike the positive association between silence and expectation ("Vida entera," p. 35 above), in the climax of "Huerto de Melibea," Guillén joins silence and universal anticipation to dramatize the impact of negative impulses on life and love.

As in the poems which were chosen to open this discussion of love and silence, strains from *Cántico* re-appear in other contexts to muffle the dissonance in *Clamor*. One such example, "Tréboles" (pp. 1006-1007), re-states the theme of silence as a protective layer among the levels of friendship and meaningful conversation:

> Placer de hablar: amigos somos,
> Aunque los temas evitados
> Formen silencio en muchos tomos.
> Es el día del Señor.
> Suene música sagrada.
> Cántico sobre clamor.

> (1006: 12;   1007: 1)

The un-spoken dialogues contain both subjects to be avoided and tacit agreements. But if there is to be genuine humanity, one must choose to cultivate the levels of affect which can be shared. Even when there are overtones of bitterness and disappointment, the comfort of familiar contacts may lead to renewed creativity: "Noche, plomo, noche. / Pase. / Algo saldrá a su mañana, / Al ímpetu de una frase." ("Tréboles", 1009: 11.) [29]

C. *Homenaje.*

The continuity of Guillén's poetic vision is perhaps best appreciated in the light of *Homenaje.* [30] With respect to the contexts of silence and love, the third book of *Aire nuestro* impressively unfolds the coherence and vitality of Guillén's perspectivistic art.

"El lenguaje del amor" (p. 1309) takes the theme and point of view of poetic recreation as one of the most rewarding en-

---

[29] The structure and style of the numerous "Tréboles" in *Aire nuestro* warrant a more detailed study than could be attempted in this book. The arrangement of these poems within a specific division of *Aire nuestro* as well as their thematic and stylistic relationship with the surrounding poems deserve a separate analysis.

[30] Ricardo Gullón, "*Homenaje* con variaciones," 6, makes this point convincingly.

deavors. The poem, which is itself a transformation of experience, re-awakens the pulse and uniqueness of love:

> Desemboca el silencio en la palabra,
> Y la palabra surge
> Con tal fervor que es nueva
> Para nombrarte, desnudez presente
> Bajo la luz que te descubre, pura,
> En un retiro exento
> De sombra hacia pecado,
> Sin ese vil espejo que deforme,
> Tendido en su lenguaje por los otros,
> Tu intimidad, amor,
> Siempre recién creada: poesía.

Out of silent, lucid gestation, the metamorphosis of experience through language comes to creative realization. Not as a substitute for original love but as a tribute to love's resistance, the intimate recreation generates new feeling and renewed depth. The poem thus re-defines the radius of love in time and space.

On a more concrete level, silence tinctures the everyday needs of love with a similar vitality. The sharing of silence, in love-making or in sleep, restores energy and enthusiasm. In the separate sleep of "Tregua de la inquietud", p. 1629, the lovers re-charge their connectedness: "Duermen. Dos sueños. Y armonizan. Helos / Tejiendo su silencio serio a tono / Con los astros: destino sin pregunta." Each one remains fully himself, but the shared experience silently deepens the couple's understanding. The commitment to love well respects the need to restore and refresh its ties: "Entre mi boca y tu boca / Triunfe el silencio mayor." ("Lenguaje," p. 1428.) In this accommodation ego and alterity seek the level of harmonious love:

> Conjunción oscura,
> Acorde en silencio.
> Dos fuerzas se entienden
> Ya también personas,
> Ellas son... nosotros
> En cúspide amante,
> Tan protagonistas
> Aunque espectadores.
> Nosotros: veraz
> Teatro de amor.
>
> ("Repertorio de Junio," no. 18, p. 1362)

The simple adjustment between subject and object which is essential if relationship is to occur, remains at the core of Guillén's most recent love poetry. As a basic lesson, it is not a context which suffers from thoughtful repetition.

Given the centrality of silence as a complement to loving, it is natural to conceive of it as a conductor for sexual impulse: "En los ojos la pasión. / En la boca los instintos / Más torpes y oscuros con / Silencios de saña tintos. / Así somos, ay, perdón." ("Cara," p. 1262.) [31] Silence is such an intimate companion to love that it becomes synonymous with the beloved: "Tanto silencio en torno tuyo," and it confirms her place in the world: "Y a través de lo oscuro, tú, criatura, clave." ("Amor a Silvia," no. 60, p. 1351.) To recognize where and how love enriches life, is to become a silent love poet:

> No te comparo a la flor.
> Eres sin nombre tú misma.
> ¡Oh capital de mi culto!
> Mi destino en ti se abisma.
> Sea el silencio en tu honor.

("Amor a Silvia," no. 20, p. 1363)

The contrast in diction between the third and final verses delightfully suggests the limits of language and the value of silence. This explains why the lover's highest praise singles out the beauty of love's vibrant silence: "Te llamo desde lo oscuro, / Y tu nombre va a la sombra. / Noche con hondo silencio / Me dice amor: tu respuesta." ("Jaculatorias," p. 1660). [32]

---

[31] Related contexts of love's silence in *Homenaje*: pp. 1200, 1365, 1428, 1435.

[32] Other instances of the silence of the beloved: pp. 1361, 1430; the motif of silence and friendship is also important in "Invitación a un viaje," 1307:1, and "Azorín," III, 1505:1.

IV

NEGATIVE SILENCES

The moods and faces of silence are as varied as the human settings in which they are perceived. But more important than the diversity of contextual data are the perspectives which Guillén's dialectical language brings into focus. Because *Aire nuestro* is a creative matrix of correspondence and contrast, the full spectrum of silence, its blackness as well as its transparency, colors the poetic development. The knowledge of how silence comes to be associated with negative situations, and the way it exacerbates hostility or de-humanization is what enables Guillén to exploit its connotative richness.

A considerable portion of twentieth-century Spanish poetry concerns itself with the negativities of contemporary life, and, most emphatically, with the expression of alienation in a hostile world. [33] Some of Guillén's explicit beliefs and attitudes converge with the fundamental tenets of the radical esthetic in poetry. [34] The "Hollow men" whose spectres appear in the poetry of Alberti, who populate the frozen planet of Lorca's New York, Neruda's *Residencias*, and Dámaso Alonso's islands of despair, also emerge on the scene of Guillén's "Ciudad doliente". What distinguishes Guillén's outrage from that of most of his contemporaries is the multiplicity of angles and the underlying

---

[33] C. B. Morris, *A Generation of Spanish Poets*, pp. 143-232; Paul Ilie, *The Surrealist Mode*, pp. 80-104, et passim.

[34] Debicki, *Estudios*, pp. 49-51; Eugenio Frutos, "El existencialismo jubiloso de Jorge Guillén," *CHA*, 18 (1950), 411-426; Jorge Guillén, *Language and Poetry*, pp. 201-204; C. B. Morris, pp. 121-142.

cultural pluralism which he brings to the problems of today. This difference is most apparent in Guillén's concept of history and its relationship to the human condition. Unlike the ideological bias of Neruda or Alonso, Guillén separates the question of man's existence from the events which dramatize his historical moment. Consequently, he does not place the burden of blame for man's failures on the course of history. He assumes it to be everyone's task to break the destructive pattern of events, and thus define man's responsibility and create his role in history: "La historia es sólo voluntad del hombre." (p. 1043:26.)

More often than not, the contextual frame of Guillén's ideological poetry is dialectical or ironic. For this reason, there is a tight connection between poems which are explicitly political in character and those which do not develop a concrete, historical situation. In other words, the humanism and artistic play of *Cántico* and *Homenaje* are integrated in the historical content of *Clamor*. Together, the three books make up a sliding mirror in which no angle of focus excludes the essential human reality. Seen in this light, no one act excludes the aggregate: collective disasters have their individual counterparts; national errors of judgment are each citizen's mistake. On all levels of existence, mindless conformity and indifference are weapons of destruction not far removed from the tyrant's arsenal. In another joint perspective, the duplicity of a single individual perpetrates the state's corruption. There is no historical time — even when freedom and health are most securely institutionalized — that a culture can afford to stop the course of criticism and concern. Silence weighs heavily in human dialectics: it tests and even undermines the actions behind man's words, the humanity in his abstractions.

A. *Cántico*

In a range of negativity, the contexts of silence in *Cántico* occupy a fringe area. But implicit in the book's dominant tone there are negative resonances: interstices of pain, troubled sleep, fragmentation of experience, unsettling thoughts. *Cántico*, like all of Guillén's poetry, is not of a piece; it is no endless existential fiesta. Doubts about the possibility of meaningful life, moments of intellectual or emotional blocking, frustration and failure are woven into its fabric. It is basically in the preceding net of circumstances where silence becomes painful, astringent, or inhuman.

Since there is often a thin line between the affirmations of a confident being and the anxiety of another, Guillén sees in the zones of ambivalence opportunities to come to grips with some of man's most pressing preoccupations. He also brings to these dilemmas an open-mindedness and humor which serve to erase the false thinking in their original formulation. While the point is obviously to have fun at the expense of pseudo-intellectuals, other contexts aim at the nature and validity of contradiction. In this case, Guillén makes creative room for paradox, inconsistency, and tension in the gamut of human problems.

Dreams, and the fuzzy states before awakening are particularly rich material for the play of dialectics or irony. The distortions and underlying order of dreams point up the simultaneity of assertion and contradiction, the paradoxes which clarify rather than mystify. In this sense, the content and analysis of dreams is an excellent starting point for creative thinking. Several poems in *Cántico* are just that: dream-pieces, explicated in the first-person or by an authoritative intermediary.

"Los sueños buscan" (p. 329), for example, depicts the potential terror of dead silence in a dreamer's labyrinth: "¿Los sueños buscan el mayor peligro? / ... / ¿Así tú, caminante sin oriente, / Avanzarás hasta perderte, niño? / Copas, troncos te aguardan con silencio / Mortal... No. ¡Grita, rómpelo! Y el bosque / Te acogerá con un rumor amigo." [35] Both the inquisitive tone and the future tense supply a positive point of view in the landscape of nightmare, and the unanswered questions come to a grinding halt with the key word, "mortal". Dead silence is broken by the human voice and restored to its familiar tones.

A similar shift in perspective turns on the appearances of imminent destruction:

> ¿Tan turbia es nuestra incertidumbre
> Que ni un rayo habrá que la alumbre?
> El mundo se inclina a su muerte.

---

[35] Casalduero considers the deliberate break in tone of this text characteristic of Guillén's affirmative poetic reality (*Jorge Guillén*, p. 120). Cf. Ricardo Gullón, "La poesía de Jorge Guillén," p. 72.

> Hasta el silencio está roído
> Por algún fantasma de ruido
> Que en sordo abuso lo convierte...

How does one find evidence of stability in such a chaos of natural phenomena?

> ¿Todo morirá en mala bruma?
> No, no, no. Vencerá la Tierra,
> Que en firmamento nos encierra:
> Ya al magno equilibrio nos suma.
> ("Estación del norte," 378:19; 379:18)

The danger signs are only dislodged halves of the picture. When placed in the context of totality, they are components of an order. The erosion of silence by "algún fantasma de ruido" certainly suggests the final stage of cosmic break-down: when silence has been banished, chaos must be imminent. But like the contradictory meaning of "sordo abuso", both phenomena are only half-glimpsed stages in the process of accommodation. Thus, the division of the poem into two distinct perspectives — the first, realistically described, but falsely perceived; the second, generalized and interpretative — serves a dialectical plan. The leap in thought and meaning which seems to take place between the two separate perspectives has in fact been bridged by the rhetorical questions and the final denial. While the tension between destruction and creation has been poetically knit in this poem, Guillén's alternate technique is to pursue an opposition, to allow the full dynamics of discontinuity. The poem, "Silencio en el origen," p. 1253, is a good example of the tension which remains after the play of apparent conflict.

"Anulación de lo peor," p. 333, is structurally related to the other poems I have brought into this discussion. While there is more attention to imagery, the poem works out a synthesis from extreme perspectives:

> Sin luces, ya nocturna toda, bárbara,
> En torno a los silencios encrespándose,
> La noche con sus bestias aulladoras se yergue.

The uneasy sleeper is locked in a landscape of terror; a scene made more impressive by the synesthesias he perceives: light, sound, and forms merge into a single nocturnal horror.

¿Una aprensión te angustia?
No temas.

Los aullidos,
El mal con sus galápagos, sus gárgolas,
Noche abajo enfangándose, cayendo,
En noche se trasfunden. La noche toda es fondo.
Espera, pues.

El sol descubrirá,
Bellísima inocente, la simple superficie.

The poem is a kaleidescopic paradigm, more like an unfinished abstract than a surrealist's canvas. [36] It describes what happens when one focuses prematurely on an object. The initial verses, and the qualification which follows their description, introduce conflicting perceptions of a single phenomenon. The frightened viewer projects his anxiety, and anticipates chaos; while the third-person intermediary views the scene from the angles of its flux. Because night is in the process of daymaking it is too soon ("espera, pues") to predict the outcome; and the stages of unfinished work do present strange configurations ("los aullidos, el mal," etc.). With the coming of dawn, organicity, beauty, and the familiar will be restored.

A delicate complement to the resonances of this poem is very simply stated in "Lo esperado" (p. 101):

Después de tantas noches
Arqueadas en túneles
De una luna entre roces
De silencio y de nube,

Aquí está lo esperado.
El doliente vacío
Va poblándose. ¡Pájaros!

The rhythm of seasons, like the process of day-break, has an order which balances and makes tolerable the stages of apparent negativity.

---

[36] J. M. Blecua construes this poem as "surrealistic," and, therefore, atypical of Guillén's esthetic ("En torno a *Cántico*," in *La poesía de Jorge Guillén*, p. 219).

B. *Clamor*

The sub-title of *Clamor*, "Tiempo de Historia," announces Guillén's choice of poetic frame, but its meaning is deliberately ambiguous. Is this poetry concerned with a particular epoch ("Time of History"), or is it about the special temporality of historical events ("History's Time")? Because context is so crucial to an understanding of Guillén's poetry, the study of one conceptual core can bring to light the meanings of another. The silence which is so deeply embedded in the pages of *Clamor* affords the opportunity to hear the overtones in "Tiempo de Historia."

Although the style of *Clamor* is less metaphoric and more densely narrative than the idiom of *Cántico* or *Homenaje*, its expressive range is not limited to a single mode of discourse. The orchestration of points of view, and the levels of consciousness explored necessarily produce stylistic variety. But *Clamor* is marked by the language of history, too; its voice comes from and speaks with the contemporary world. There are sharp vocalizations and pensive moods which carry the poet's reactions and ideas. These underlying values mesh in the development of theme. Thus, the negative contexts of silence in *Clamor* embrace the term's cumulative meanings and expand its associations through Guillén's poignant understanding of our "Tiempo de Historia."

The futility of war occasions one of Guillén's most impassioned reactions. The imagery of "Guerra en la paz" (pp. 692-698), like the semantic distortions it employs, mirrors the chaos and pain of unnecessary conflict. Modern warfare is a "Calvario de una nada / Que el hombre inventaría." (696:18.) The language of paradox conveys the inverted rationale of war: "Ruptura de universo. / ¿La Tierra será el astro / De la estulticia trágica?" (697:3.) The silence which precedes the attack by "Satán atómico" swells and re-echoes in the after-math:

> Un clamor se articula
> Dentro de los silencios reunidos.
> Cambiante, la Amenaza se oscurece
> Bajo el sol: suplemento
> De nube dirigida.
> ¿Impersonal, anónima?
> ¿O desde una ventana se la impulsa

Contra el coro viviente,
Contra ti, contra mí, contra los muchos
Clamantes
En clamor silencioso?

(697:6)

The self-generating momentum of war takes the place of human choice and responsibility, and the silence of the multitudes is the reason for being of their leaders:

Son los más. Y se callan.
Son los más, tan correctos,
Sumisos a los pocos, invisibles,
A los muy pocos. ¿Mágicos?

(697:17)

Inertia and conformism are the real evils, not the concentration of power. Through silent approval, the majority yields control to a few individuals. The result of this co-option is self-defeating: a rule of brutality, and non-leaders ("invisibles," "mágicos") whose stupidity destroys civilized life.

"Potencia de Pérez" is Guillén's longest poem of moral outrage; it begins the drama of modern dictatorship where "Guerra en la paz" ends. Instead of presenting a single narrative line, Guillén mounts a split stage on which the tragedy of collective silence and the political farce are jointly enacted. This dramatic doubling of perspectives gives the poem greater artistic latitude than the contents of its message.

As in the last-mentioned text, the origin of organized madness can be traced to collective silence: "¿Disidente? Ninguno / Que no sea culpable. / Diferir es manchar la gran blancura / De la Historia aclarada. / ¿Y el pensamiento bajo su silencio? / Preferible el disfraz. / Mentid." (575:14.) People cannot remain 'politically pure' without thereby sanctioning what they purport to oppose. Once the potential to resist has been smothered by hypocrisy, any real sense of outrage can only echo in subterranean silence: "...Cantad con energía, / Cantad. / El país es el coro de los coros." (575:23.)

In this climate of mute acquiescence, minds and sensibilities atrophy:

¿Aquel semblante escucha?
Un pensamiento al fin sin pensamiento

Corona
La siesta de una oreja adormecida.
¿Qué verdad clausurada no adormece?
No, no difiera nadie.

(579:11)

No one hears the senseless oratory; no one needs to think in a
pre-programmed game. But the political arena of the oppressor
has one exit, and, inevitably, it is the same mute majority who
will not escape with their lives. One of the last tableaux in
"Potencia de Pérez" depicts the mannequin's triumph. A gro-
tesque emptiness, "figura sin figura," Pérez is nevertheless the
'power' behind the devastation:

Ensangrentado Pérez bien ungido,
Tan dueño del presente,
Un presente muy largo sin futuro
De historia que no aboque a la catástrofe.
Todos la temen, nadie la desea:
Que el tirano persista.

(585:6)

As Pérez oversees his "artilugio triunfal," the future has already
been cancelled:

Se adivina latente
Clamor con un furor
Que llenará de espanto
La escena de la farsa:
Muertos y muertos, muertos.

(585:20)

In this context of nullifying silence, one of the principal meanings
of "Tiempo de Historia" is fused: man's individual history has
become "presentes sucesiones de difunto." "Potencia de Pérez"
occupies the same tundra as Martínez Santos' *Tiempo de silencio*; both works record the spectacle of total eclipse in which
man subverts his humanity through acts of negation. [37]

Not all historical crises end in impotence. For Guillén, the
commitment of youth to defy repression is one antidote to
the complicity of the silent majority:

---

[37] Ricardo Gullón draws a parallel with *Tiempo de silencio* and the
film techniques of Bergman in "Persona," ("*Homenaje* con variaciones," 6).
Related contexts of negative silence in *Clamor*: pp. 593, 857, 959.

Un relámpago, de pronto,
Convierte el silencio en trance
De rumor que es choque y lucha.
Las esperanzas combaten
A los solemnes embustes,
Y puños de mocedades
Esgrimen Historia clara
Que ilumina porque arde.

("Los hijos," 717:13)

In the center of this poem, the negative silence of disillusion and despair ("Guerra en la Paz," "Potencia de Pérez") has been filled with youth's vibrant promise. Similarly, the associations for "Historia" are diametrically opposed to the preceding ones: a live, hopeful history crushes the forces of de-humanization.

The time of sanctioned disorder figures as an important context for the action of negative silence. The longest poem in "Maremágnum," "Luzbel desconcertado" (pp. 604-625), develops the idea of chaos as a 'superior system.' But the irony and theatricality with which Guillén handles the subject make this poem a self-destructing monologue. Isolated from the reality of others, the protagonist rationalizes his egotism: "Vigila tus silencios hasta / Que sean oro. / Jamás descubras tu tesoro: / Sé un alma casta. / Honor a la esterilidad / Del exquisito, / Inexpugnable en su Infinito. / ¡Callad, callad!" (611:5.) Order, harmony, humanity, and beauty either bore or repel the devil: "Armonía, prisión / Dorada. / ¿No es el mayor escándalo?" (613:1.) He thrives in the urban tumult and hostility: "Me siento alegre en esta batahola / De la ciudad. / Estrépito, / Contradicción, contraste, mediodía / Del sol sobre los ruidos." (613:25.) Knowing the meaning of creative silence, he longs for an ear-splitting discharge of noise and pain: "¡Clamor! / Clamor doliente de los más opresos, / Clamor sin llanto de los capitanes, / Clamor de muchos, muchos tan perdidos / Que ni saben de tantos / Ya perdidos, su propia muchedumbre, / Clamor con rabia oscura o claridad / Rabiosa,..." (615:8.) Silence is an adversary of the devil's cause; he understands its unifying power. Only as in the opening verses, in its condition as a frozen ground for the imprisoned ego, does silence figure as a part of dehumanization in this poem.

The crisis of inversion calls for a new humanism, an antidote to the sterility and the consequences of hubris. Guillén's lucid dialogue, "Como tú, lector" (pp. 1050-1051), contrasts in every way with the world of the preceding poem. In its direct appeal and simplicity, there is a deep concern: "El hombre se cansa de ser cosa, la cosa que / sirve sabiéndose cosa, cosa de silencio en su po- / tencia de impulso airado. La hombría del hom- / bre, de muchos hombres se cansa atrozmente." The message has been translated many times in recent years: under the surface silence of the oppressed there is an explosive anger. The responsibility to convert this energy into constructive acts is the first priority: "Es crisis de Historia" (p. 1050:20). The question is one of choosing between opposing times: the tyranny of silent time versus the compassion of personal time. [38]

> Deja de leer, mira los visillos de la ventana...
> A ti también te anuncia la catástrofe de las
> catástrofes. ¿Terminará la esclavitud? ¿Hombres
> habrá que no sean cosas? Hombres como tú,
> lector, sentado en tu silla. Nada más.
>
> (1051: 13)

C. *Homenaje*

Whereas the contexts of negative silence in *Clamor* reflect moral outrage, the range of meanings in *Homenaje* has a psychological basis. The communications that fail to take place, the denial of self and others, and the pain of irrationality combine to create a poetry about personal isolation. This sense of fragmentation is expressed in Guillén's question, "¿Un mudo tiempo inmenso nos divide...?" [39] Unlike the definitive separations which conflict produces, the isolations in *Homenaje* are interludes in a wider panorama of sharing and mutual respect. *Homenaje* is by definition a celebration of human and literary affinities: the contexts of negativity are therefore sparse in its total expression.

For a study in the experience of dissociation, "El monstruo" (p. 1606) offers a useful lesson: "¡Si te arrojase, monstruo / Que desde el interior / Del silencio me afliges y torturas, / Si te arrojase en una vomitona / Del alma!" The belief that something

---

[38] Similar referents for silence: pp. 514, 589, 941.

[39] "Encuentro final," p. 1406. For a survey of the poetry on the subject of incommunicability, see C. B. Morris, pp. 144-145, 207-241.

alien to one's self has invaded and taken control of the former inhabitant is a common symptom of schizophrenia. [40] In this poem, however, a timely realization thwarts the action of personality splitting: "Pero el alma no cuenta con tentáculos / De expulsión imperiosa, / Y sufre resistiendo / Tanta desarmonía, / Ya un monstruo. / ¿Será quizá... yo mismo?" The monster is an auto-creation. The restoration of equilibrium comes from tenacious self-criticism.

Even when we learn how not to be our own worst enemy, there are times when one's resources are depleted and human contact is the most pressing need:

> Este silencio atroz me desespera,
> Y ser no puede un desenlace humano.
> No retorne mi mano ya a tu mano.
> Que suene una palabra verdadera.
>
> La boca muda permanece fuera
> Del día hermoso por el que me afano:
> Don de espíritu en forma sin arcano
> Muy confuso de tácita sordera.
>
> Yo necesito oír una palabra,
> Aunque ninguna puerta ya me abra,
> Y quede errando a solas por la calle.
>
> Es todo preferible a la tortura
> De afrontar esa nada tan oscura
> Que me fuerza a morir, a que me calle.

("Contra el silencio," p. 1436)

In this sonnet, as in a prison of solitary confinement, painful silence reaches its peak. For the speaker, nothing human can take place in his world because he views his connectedness with others as a severed limb. The disjointed imagery of the quatrains mirrors the action of despair on all the senses. The sharp difference in tone and point of view which distinguishes the tercets from the preceding verses implies an interlude during which the speaker has made a break-through: he accepts the fact of his dependence on

---

[40] R. D. Laing, *The Divided Self* (Baltimore: Pelican, 1968), Chapters 3-8.

others as a self-preserving option, and the understanding that he can reverse the course of alienation will lead to a direct action.

The solution enacted in "Contra el silencio" is pitted against its undoing in a similarly entitled sonnet, "Sin diálogo" (p. 1426). Frozen in the isolation of his own fictions, the monologuist resembles the victim of "silencio atroz":

> Monólogos, monólogos tenaces
> Acoge soledad tan desmedida
> Que sufres el silencio como herida,
> Más dolorosa porque la rehaces.
>
> ¿Prefieres tus discursos a las paces,
> Y tu espejo será quien te decida
> Tristemente a elegir la hostil huída
> Por el vacío donde te complaces?
>
> Habla o grita o resurge en estallido
> De cólera hacia un aire articulado.
> Caótico es un orden siempre interno.
>
> ¿No habrás de dar a tu actitud sentido?
> ¿No es el mudo un horrible condenado?
> ¿No quieres escaparte de tu infierno?

In radical isolation, the "yo" perceives himself as the most desirable interlocutor, thereby insulating a precarious idea of his reality from actual contact. While he goes through the motions of self-assertion, the counter-action of "un orden siempre interno" undermines his identity and forces him to suffer repeated despair. The speaker's advice points to the obvious cure: relationship heals and gives life to the otherwise futile gestures of a shadow. It is a very effective device in this sonnet that the subject, the "yo" who has sealed off his humanity, remains silent. His implied presence, however, becomes intensified in the quatrains. A line of empty substantives leaves the most hollow imprint: "monólogos," "soledad," "silencio;" "discursos," "espejo," "huída," "vacío." In contrast, the speaker's compassion is expressed in a thrust of verbs: "habla," "grita," "resurge;" "habrás de dar," "quieres escaparte." A human being's presence resonates in the tercets against the static shell of the victim's de-humanization.

V

METAPHYSICAL SILENCE

While silence is a vibrant presence in the world and our representations of reality, it is not a tangible phenomenon; it must be endowed with form and meaning independent of its perceived qualities. A poetics of silence, like a philosophy which asserts its ontological status, aims to concretize what is by nature metaphysical. Studies in mythology, philosophy, and poetics have proposed solid interpretations for the esthetic and phenomenological contexts of silence. [41] Their differing concepts and perspectives converge on one of man's perennial aspirations: to integrate transcendence in theories of knowledge.

Although Guillén may be said to have provided an idiom for the qualities of silence, both the language and its expression are esthetic. This is not to disclaim philosophical implications in the poet's creation. At least two-thirds of the fore-going analysis of silence reveals to what extent Guillén's poetry is concerned with modes of awareness, knowledge, and speech. Nevertheless, the realities of experience in *Aire nuestro* are not subordinate to an ultimate reality. No attempt is made to formulate a hierarchy of experience; the sublime and the prosaic surface over the everyday lens through which the world is perceived. Creative ordering of the real and the potential is Guillén's answer to vital human prob-

---

[41] John Cage, *Silence* (M. I. T. Press, 1966); Ernst Cassirer, *Language and Myth*, trans. Susanne K. Langer (New York: Dover, 1953), pp. 62-74; Max Picard, *The World of Silence*, especially, pp. 15-35, 72-81, 113-122, 136-160, 211-231; Jerzy Pietrkiewicz, *The Other Side of Silence* (London: Oxford University Press, 1970), pp. 1-16, 69-75, et passim.

lems; but it is an artistic answer which does not constitute a final or systematic expression. Guillén recognizes that silence extends beyond man's concrete experience, yet his poetry affirms how its resonances in the world enhance and re-define that essential concreteness. Through the intervention of the poet, the tangible and the intangible cohere.

The interlocking universe of *Aire nuestro* grows into and nurtures whatever genuine spirituality man may invent or discover. In terms of Guillén's poetics, the world of silence implies metaphysics. To perceive silence as harmony, to live creatively or in pain its effects on human endeavor, is to place a transcendent value on the way silence reverberates in man's total existence. It is therefore symptomatic of Guillén's poetic vision that the principal metaphysical contexts of silence in *Aire nuestro* refer to time, ideal beauty, and death. This contextual core of silence represents experience which gives us esthetic models: in metaphysical silence we make and appreciate the real "aire nuestro" which is ontological creativity.

A. *Cántico*

Beauty is not a fixed criterion. It is a dynamic recognition: the moment when theory and practice synchronize in creative perception. In "El arco de medio punto" (p. 235), close attention to the details of an historical development in architecture leads the observer to understand natural and created unity:

> Muro a muro, hueco a hueco,
> La Historia es este descanso
> Donde opera aún el eco
> De una gran voz, hoy ya manso
> Discurrir de una armonía
> Presente. La galería
> Conduce hasta el gran conjunto,
> Que muda todo sol en
> Luz serena. ¡Mira bien
> El arco de medio punto!

The Roman arch relates so perfectly with the surrounding space ("muro," "hueco," "galería," "conjunto") that it projects perfect harmony. The semi-silent voice resonates in the now which is all time. [42] Oppositions are resolved in the total context: sound, silence, light, shadow, filled and empty space fuse in a single archetype of beauty.

A similar revelation of formal beauty structures the poem, "Vida extrema" (pp. 398-405). In terms of technique and focus, this poem identifies the process of perceptual insights: "Una metamorfosis necesita / Lo tan vivido pero no acabado, / Que está exigiendo la suprema cita: / Encarnación en su perenne estado." (II, 399:5.) There are no beginnings or endings in creative life; moments of illumination capture the essential happenning. Thus, the task of poetry is to find a correlative for the intuitive understanding of the world: "¿Quién tu sentido, Globo, te adivina?" (400:12.) Out of the sounds and sights of reality's flux, pattern emerges: "Poesía forzosa. De repente, / Aquella realidad entonces santa, / A través de la tarde trasparente, / Nos desnuda su esencia. ¿Quién no canta?" (403:13.) The expressive vehicle for this insight is like' the poem itself: it illuminates the simultaneity of concept and creative awareness. This privileged moment eludes time and chance:

> Atención nada más de buen amigo.
> Nació ya, nacerá. ¡Infiel, la gloria!
> Mejor el buen silencio que consigo
> Resguarda los minutos sin historia.
>
> (403:21)

Silence shares in the process of artistic synthesis because it is itself an act of listening and translation.

Almost all of the metaphysical implications of silence which Guillén develops appear in the poem "Arena" (p. 492). It is a stunning synthesis of tangible and intangible realities. The poem has a tight binary structure, underscored in the typographical division. The first part recreates the perennial action of ocean and beach; a dramatic cacophony underlines the meaning. [43] The

---

[42] See González Muela's close reading of "El arco de medio punto," in *La realidad y Jorge Guillén*, pp. 198-199.

[43] The phonetic structure of "Arena" has been described by Oreste Macrí, "Phono-symbolism in *Cántico*," trans. Ivar Ivask, in "An International Symposium in Honor of Jorge Guillén at 75," *BA*, 42 (Winter, 1968), 50.

tensioned noise is followed by a single word, "¿Paz?," which marks the break in tone and content of what follows:

> Y una ola
> Pequeña cae sin ruido
> Sobre la arena, suave
> De silencio. ¡Qué alivio,
> Qué sosiego, silencio
> De siempre, siempre antiguo!
> Porque Dios, sin edad,
> Tiene ante sí los siglos.
> Sobre la arena duran
> Calladamente limpios.
> Retumbe el mar, no importa.
> El silencio allí mismo.

In the layers of silence there is an accumulated meaning. Sand, sound, time, and sea are united in a cyclical image of eternity. In this context, Guillén's technique of objectification makes silence an autonymous phenomenon and a transcendent quality. The implied speaker affirms this identification in the logical flow of his observation ("Porque Dios..., Tiene ante sí los siglos"), and in the serene confidence of his reflection, "no importa." The sands which preserve time are themselves imbued with silence; like the centuries which stretch out before God, silence comprises permanence and infinity.

Rather than a horizontal projection of metaphysical silence, Guillén takes a geometric image in "Gran silencio" (p. 325):

> Gran silencio. Se extiende a la redonda
> La infinitud de un absoluto raso.
> Una sima sin fin horada el centro.
> Y sin cesar girando cae, cae,
> Ya invisible y zumbón, celeste círculo.

Symbolically, the circle holds and buzzes with harmony; it is, as Morris suggests, a reassuring image of harmony in the world. [44]

---

[44] Useful studies on Guillén's poetization of the circle include: C. B. Morris, pp. 125-126; Eugenio Frutos, "The Circle and its Rupture in the Poetry of Jorge Guillén," trans. Ivar Ivask, in "An International Symposium," 33-36; George McSpadden, "New Light on Speech Rhythms from Jorge Guillén's Reading of His Poem 'Gran Silencio'," HR, XXX (July, 1962), 217-218.

The concrete and the abstract are brought together in the context of ideal wholeness. A similar perception of the mysterious unity of space and silence provides the beautiful synesthesias of "Noche planetaria," p. 512:

> A estas horas lentísimas
> Sólo en la noche queda
> Vacío en vibración...
> Pululación en torno,
> Que al oído rodea
> De un susurro en el límite
> De la noche y su niebla
> De realidad, ahora
> Más que nunca ligera,
> Cuando lo más desierto
> Se resuelve en materia
> Posible de Infinito,
> Y ya casi resuena
> Con nada que lo es todo.
>
> Silencio
> de planeta.

The vibrations of silence are charged with potentiality. In the pulse-like texture of night, the universe sketches its tenuous outline. What appears most insubstantial ("vacío en vibración," "pululación," "límite de la noche," "niebla de realidad," "lo más desierto," "Infinito," "nada") becomes proof of permanent reality. Silence synthesizes totality and nothingness for the responsive artist whose medium is the cosmos. [45]

B. *Clamor*

"Lugar de Lázaro" and "Huerto de Melibea" are, respectively, the opening and closing selections in the second part of *Clamor*, "... Que van a dar en la mar." Structurally, they may be considered reflective supports for the more than two-hundred poems which they enclose. "Huerto de Melibea" is Guillén's most sustained lyric poem in dramatic form; "Lugar de Lázaro" may be thought of as its narrative counterpart. The latter dramatizes

---

[45] Related contexts in *Cántico*: pp. 301, 357, 430, 512, 530-531.

a miraculous act of divine love; the former enacts the play of an all-too-human one. Both pieces reveal a density of imagistic silence. The sensual concretization of silence in "Huerto de Melibea" has its contrastive side in the spiritual connotations which the term acquires in "Lugar de Lázaro." [46]

"Lugar de Lázaro" consists of four parts of varying length which externalize the drama of death and resurrection. A long discursive passage explains Lázaro's consciousness in death and foreshadows the miracle. His silent conformity with the will of God speaks for his absolute faith: "¡Qué pureza / Terrible, qué sosiego permanente, / Espíritu en la paz que aguarda al Hijo!" (I, 737:26.) Knowing the limits of endurance, "El Señor decidió entonces / Asistir al tan borroso." (738:1.) The will of God envelops the scene as a pregnant silence: His gift of life:

> Marta, María, las gentes
> Lloran entre sus sollozos,
> Y el Hijo del Hombre llora
> Con un llanto silencioso.
>
> (739:10)

Spiritual silence fills the gap between human and divine knowledge, while the unsharable silence rings with His secret: "un duelo a punto de ser / Convertido en gran asombro." (739:8.) Later, when Lázaro resumes life on earth, he brings the Other Silence with him:

> Lázaro está ya siendo el nuevo Lázaro
> Después de su aventura.
> Con modestia sonríe entre los suyos,
> A quienes nada tiene que contar.
> ¿Supo? ¿Qué supo? ¿Sabe?
> Lo sabe sin palabras,
> Sin referencias a comunes términos
> Humanos.
> ¿Preguntan? Nada dice.
>
> (741:1)

---

[46] The dramatic structure of "Lugar de Lázaro" has been sketched by J. M. Caballero Bonald, "Un nuevo adelanto de *Clamor*," *PSA*, VI (1957), 329-333. Cf. Joaquín Casalduero, "'Lugar de Lázaro'," trans. Ivar Ivask, in "An International Symposium," 23-25.

Lázaro's silence, the incommunicable language of God with man, is now his unique wisdom. Having experienced the Final Silence, he must make a return to the world of words: "... vivir es siempre cotidiano, / Y volver a vivir se aprende pronto." (741:12.) The matter-of-fact tone serves as a fitting contrast to the metaphysical purport of the secret wisdom. The opposition is resolved in the daily familiarity of Lázaro's community, all is clear, everything relates: "Y la voz de María, / Y el silencio de Marta, / Que se escucha también, / Y pesa. / Todo es sencillo y tierno..." (742:5.)

But in the most real terms, Lázaro's knowledge and experience do separate his humanity from that of his fellow mortals: "De paz no goza el hombre que recuerda / Para sí, para dentro, lo indecible. / Único en el retorno de ultratumba, / Se interroga, compara, sufre, teme, / Se encomienda a su Dios, / Suplica." (746:19.) Having heard the ultimate silence, Lázaro longs to return to the source of that miracle. The final portion of the poem states his paradox:

> Privilegiado me yergo
> Frente a ese mundo que ignora
> Cuánto me enseñó un silencio.
>
> (747:8)

Accepting the mystery which divides his knowledge in this world from spiritual revelation, Lázaro humbly awaits his next fate.

In addition to the eschatological contexts of silence in "Lugar de Lázaro" there are several other poems in *Clamor* which develop the association of silence with timelessness and death. "Perspectivas con fuentes," for example, might be considered the esthetic companion piece to "El arco de medio punto" and "Arena" in *Cántico*. The admiring spectator in an Italian garden invites the reader to share his experience of natural and formal beauty. Fountains, landscaping, statues, and towering cypresses harmonize in the continuous present: "concierto presente." Immersed in the coming-together of time and sensation, the speaker discovers a deeper meaning:

> Los cipreses, altísimos,
> Custodian una paz que se levanta,
> Se afirma y dura, monumento aéreo.

En su interior recoge
Siglos ya remansados
Por capas silenciosas donde yace
Con vigor de reposo una reserva
De lo que fue vivido,
Profundo
Presente bajo el sol de los cipreses.

(881:20)

Time is continuous, but it may be caught in its essential duration. Through the perspective of a "sosiego de silencio" the collected monuments of time synchronize. Nothing is lost in the interlocking realities of creation, silence, and humanity. [47]

The perception of time depends on psychic scanning, how we perceive or overlook the connections between self and reality. The time-differences between subjective clockings are intensely contrastive. Harmonious time needs no justification: "Permanece mi tiempo / Todo junto en su holgura silenciosa" ("La tarde en la cima", p. 774); but awareness of how psychological time refuses to accommodate its rhythm can be a painful jolt: "... ¿No se ajustan / Los latidos del mundo a mis latidos, / Que en esta cima de la edad yo siento / Cada vez más mortales...?" (774:18.) This discrepancy echoes with the last silence: "Noche. Silencio de espada. / Y me acostumbro a la idea: / Noche, sueño, muerte, nada." ("Tréboles," 861:15.) The gamut of silence begins and ends with acuteness.

C. *Homenaje*

The inhuman silence of "Tiempo perdido," which was treated in Chapter IV of this study, contrasts sharply with the three other major divisions in this section of *Homenaje*. "Alrededor," the poem which introduces Part 4, announces the change in tone and meaning:

Llegaba hasta mí el antiguo
Relato sin voz sonante.
Deleite había en entrar
Dentro de aquellos silencios.

---

[47] A parallel context is developed in Guillén's poem, "Ciervos sobre una pared," p. 867.

Y se deslizó la pluma
Recordando, trasformando.
Era toda la persona
Quien se concentraba en voz,
La voz del nuevo relato.

(p. 1374)

Inside the cycle of silence, memory and recreation prepare the sensibilities for creative projection. These verses prefigure the central esthetic of *Homenaje*; they contain the vision of life and literature towards which many poems will gravitate. The human condition, in its shared limits and abilities, remains at the core of Guillén's recent compositions.

The other side of silence, its texture of time and death, radiates positive meaning for the present: "Desde mis propias galerías descubro firmes / itinerarios de silencio, / Y también aquel mutis en que de repente / se elude la sombra de los muertos." ("Saint-John Perse," II, 1524:13.) Guillén has a cogent exegesis on the subject of literary relevance. He takes to task the reader whose mis-guided search for his own values prevents him from experiencing the lives in literature:

A mí, lector del xx, me conturban
Los sigilosos pasos de la muerte
Que de puntillas anda "tan callando"
Tras alguien, sabe Dios, ahora mismo.

—Poesía de clase, no hay remedio.
—Hay remedio: Manrique. Con su vista
Cala mejor que tú con tus anteojos.
La clase no te deja ver al hombre.

(p. 1580)

As the title suggests, "Superación" is the ability to free one's sensibilities from self-imposed or cultural restrictions. For the unbiased reader, the "Coplas" preserve and re-activate basic human values. The reality of the poem as an historical text or a sociological model does not undermine its immediacy and universality.

Death has many faces in the tributes and evocations of *Homenaje*, but the fact of premature death gives a poignancy to many of Guillén's personal memories. In such contexts, death's piercing silence fills the space once vibrant with beautiful voices and rich conversation: "Y el silencio — mortal, incongruente, / Brusco — tajó el coloquio." ("Pedro Salinas," II, 1283 : 22.) Death as an act of silent violence is also the subject of Guillén's reaction to the murder of García Lorca: "Los muertos se extravían en silencio, / Silencio entre descargas." (III, 1291 : 13.) The black silence of assassination contrasts with the inaudible conformity of those whose death crowns a full life: "Silencioso, tranquilo agonizante, / Aguarda aquel final tan preparado / Por su guía interior: la ley se cumpla." ("Una muerte serena," p. 1386.) [48]

Birth and death, the polar silences, are only opposite points on a perfect circumference. Two important poems in *Homenaje* represent this coincidentia oppositorum. Silence is conceived as the source of life; from original purity everything can be newly born out of the fusion of opposites. "Silencio en el origen" (p. 1253) playfully formulates the dualities of this cycle:

> ¿Me zumban los oídos? ¿Es el rumor del mar?
> ¿Espacios envolventes suenan en torno nuestro?
> Ocurren los murmullos como si cabalgasen
> Jinetes invisibles, o un subsuelo de máquinas
> A compás mantuviera faena sin fatiga.
> ¿El silencio produce su aparición sonora?
> ¿Se identifican ser y nada? ¿Todo es uno?

Like a child excited before a new spectacle, the "yo" experiences delight and awe. Without stating his understanding of the process, the structure of detail and analysis grows out of a deliberate bumping of responses. The four interrogatory verses set off the imagistic center of the statement: there is a pulsating continuity in the apparent contradictions. Verses 3-5 define the coherence of earth's rhythm and change. Consequently, both pairs of questions are self-negated in the three declarative lines. What one sees beneath the surface action is a pre-view and an after-image of the underlying order.

The second poem on the subject of original silence begins where the action of the first was suspended: the world is ready to inhabit the newly created space:

---

[48] Contexts of metaphysical silence in *Homenaje*: pp. 1375, 1386, 1402, 1403, 1437, 1491, 1492, 1494, 1499.

Son tantas las dormidas soledades
En torno del amor
— invicto, vela —

Que la ciudad retorna a sus orígenes,
Reproduce el silencio aun no poblado,
Es tierra oscura que lo aguarda todo.

("Repertorio de Junio," 9, p. 1358)

Silence was there before any other concrete phenomenon; its metaphysical cycle defines its primal significance: original silence is a metaphor for the daily creation of *Aire nuestro*.

CONCLUSION

Silence fills the space and experience of *Aire nuestro*; it figures as an explicit presence in more than two hundred poems. Thus, there is hardly a single aspect of Guillén's poetic vision which does not involve the action and vibrancy of concrete silence. Its diverse contexts and perspectives give it a unique artistic and human reality. Guillén has created a world in which silence has life, and in which the full range of existence feels through silence.

Conditions of silence support peak moments: in harmonious and psychic vitality silence promotes man's alliance with the world, and the experience of its sounds and texture expands awareness and sensitivity. In its most stunning resonances, silence mediates creative and intellectual insight; it bridges the distance between the real and the ideal. But just as the whole design of *Cántico*, *Clamor*, and *Homenaje* implies the polarity of plenitude and emptiness, the contexts of silence also include negative overtones. In contrast to love's shared silence, to the new life it generates, there is exposure to violence, alienation, and loss. Negative contexts of silence sharpen the pain of human conflict. Finally, the metaphysical roots of silence deepen its reality in *Aire nuestro*. On one level, the fusion of silence with time, change, and creation gives it philosophical context; yet in another sense, the metaphorical associations with life and death humanize its paradoxical simplicity.

The lush weave of Guillén's poetry is so consistent that a single thread may carry the density of the artistic whole. And if the contexts of silence in *Cántico*, *Clamor*, and *Homenaje* reflect the poetic unity of *Aire nuestro*, will this not offer us criteria for the discovery and evaluation of other thematic cores? The unusual symbiosis of silence and esthetics is one important constant which defines Guillén's creative achievement. Others, which may apply to different motifs in *Aire nuestro*, are the poetic concretization of the intangible and its further projection to the metaphysical; the pervasive quality of silence in life; its role as a mediator in certain key human activities, such as creativity; and its reach to encompass polarized opposites.